A CHILD'S
Treasury of Verse

A CHILD'S
Treasury of Verse

Compiled by Eleanor Doan
Illustrated by Nancy Munger

ZONDERVAN PUBLISHING HOUSE

OF THE ZONDERVAN CORPORATION
GRAND RAPIDS, MICHIGAN 49506

A Child's Treasury of Verse

Copyright © 1977 by The Zondervan Corporation
Grand Rapids, Michigan
Second printing November 1977

Library of Congress Cataloging in Publication Data
Main entry under title:

A Child's treasury of verse.

  Includes indexes.
  SUMMARY: Selection topics include beauty, bits of
wisdom, friends, growing up, fun and nonsense, and talking to God.
  1. Children's poetry.   [1. American poetry — Collec-
tions]   I. Doan, Eleanor Lloyd, 1914 -   II. Munger, Nancy.
PN6110.C4C538   811'.008'0352   77-2142

ISBN 0-310-23800-5

Printed in the United States of America

Contents

I wish to acknowledge with appreciation my gratitude to

ANN WICKEY for her tireless effort in typing manuscript, indexing selections, and checking for accuracy.

MARIAN WAGENER for her interest and involvement of scores of third and fourth graders in evaluating the selections and expressing their preferences.

RUTH ROSEBERRY, especially, for her professional guidance, obtaining the participation and interest of a wide age-range of children, and encouraging young authors in their writing.

the many other teachers and children who took part in reviewing and evaluating selections so that this *Child's Treasury of Verse* will be the very best.

Dear Young Friends:

This book has been prepared just for you. It will make your life happier and more meaningful as you grow up. Each selection has been chosen with you in mind — your interests, your sense of rhythm, your growth and development, your imagination, and your love of fun.

This book spans the years of your childhood. Each year it will interest you in a new way as you read it again and again. As you do, you will

> enjoy adventure,
> develop character and Christian graces,
> laugh,
> think about happy times,
> gain wisdom,
> be grateful for your country,
> become a better person,
> and
> respond to God's love.

All the selections in this book are favorites of my many young friends across the land, and I am sure they will become your favorites too. I wish you many happy hours of enjoyment.

Your friend,
ELEANOR DOAN

Adventure

There's a place I've dreamed about
    far away
Where a tropical town crowds down
    to a bay
Busy with noise on a blowy day.

A warm mysterious coffee smell
Drifts on the air, and a singing bell
Dins and hums on a windy swell.

I've voyaged over the seven seas
In a ship that scuds before a breeze
That sounds almost like leafy trees.

When the morning is wide and
    windy and warm,
I watch that town from the tall
    yardarm
Of a poplar tree on my uncle's farm.

(Adventure)
Harry Behn

Sea-Fever

I must go down to the seas again, to
    the lonely sea and the sky,
And all I ask is a tall ship and a star to
    steer her by,
And the wheel's kick and the wind's
    song and the white sail's
    shaking
And a gray mist on the sea's face and
    a gray dawn breaking.

I must go down to the seas again, for
    the call of the running tide
Is a wild call and a clear call that may
    not be denied;
And all I ask is a windy day with the
    white clouds flying,
And the flung spray and the blown
    spume and the sea-gulls crying.

I must go down to the seas again, to
    the vagrant gypsy life,
To the gull's way and the whale's
    way where the wind's like a
    whetted knife;
And all I ask is a merry yarn from a
    laughing fellow-rover,
And quiet sleep and a sweet dream
    when the long trick's over.

John Masefield

Not of the sunlight,
Not of the moonlight,
Not of the starlight!
O young Mariner,
Down to the haven,
Call your companions,
Launch your vessel,
And crowd your canvas,
And, ere it vanishes
Over the margin,
After it, follow it,
Follow The Gleam.

Alfred Lord Tennyson
(from Merlin and the
Gleam (IX)

Travel

I should like to rise and go
Where the golden apples grow; —
Where below another sky
Parrot islands anchored lie,
And, watched by cockatoos and
    goats,
Lonely Crusoes building boats; —
Where in sunshine reaching out
Eastern cities, miles about,
Are with mosque and minaret
Among sandy gardens set,
And the rich goods from near and far
Hang for sale in the bazaar; —
Where the Great Wall round China
    goes,
And on one side the desert blows,
And with bell and voice and drum,
Cities on the other hum; —
Where are forests, hot as fire,
Wide as England, tall as a spire,
Full of apes and cocoa-nuts
And the Negro hunters' huts; —
Where the knotty crocodile
Lies and blinks in the Nile,
And the red flamingo flies
Hunting fish before his eyes; —
Where in jungles, near and far,
Man-devouring tigers are,
Lying close and giving ear
Lest the hunt be drawing near,
Or a comer-by be seen
Swinging in a palanquin; —
Where among the desert sands
Some deserted city stands,
All its children, sweep and prince,
Grown to manhood ages since,
Not a foot in street or house,
Not a stir of child or mouse,
And when kindly falls the night,
In all the town no spark of light.
There I'll come when I'm a man
With a camel caravan;
Light a fire in the gloom
Of some dusty dining-room;
See the pictures on the walls,
Heroes, fights, and festivals;
And in a corner find the toys
Of the old Egyptian boys.

Robert Louis Stevenson

Which Is the Way to Somewhere Town?

Which is the way to Somewhere
    Town?
  Oh, up in the morning early;
Over the tiles and the chimney pots,
  That is the way, quite clearly.

And which is the door to
    Somewhere Town?
  Oh, up in the morning early;
The round red sun is the door to go
    through,
  That is the way, quite clearly.

Kate Greenaway

Pussy Cat, Pussy Cat

"Pussy cat, Pussy cat,
Where have you been?"
"I've been to London
To look at the Queen."

"Pussy cat, Pussy cat,
What did you there?"
"I frightened a little mouse
Under a chair."

Christina Rossetti

The Wreck of the Hesperus

It was the schooner Hesperus,
  That sailed the wintry sea;
And the skipper had taken his little
    daughter,
  To bear him company.

Blue were her eyes, as the fairy-flax,
  Her cheeks like the dawn of day,
And her bosom white as the
    hawthorn buds,
  That ope in the month of May.

The skipper he stood beside the
    helm,
  His pipe was in his mouth;
And he watched how the veering
    flaw did blow
  The smoke now West, now South.

Then up spake an old Sailor,
  Had sailed to the Spanish Main:
"I pray thee, put into yonder port,
  For I fear a hurricane.

"Last night, the moon had a golden
    ring,
  And tonight no moon we see!"
The skipper, he blew a whiff from
    his pipe,
  And a scornful laugh laughed he.

Colder and louder blew the wind,
  A gale from the Northeast;
The snow fell hissing in the brine,
  And the billows frothed like yeast.

Down came the storm, and smote
    amain
  The vessel in its strength;
She shuddered and paused, like a
    frightened steed,
  Then leaped her cable's length.

"Come hither! come hither! my little
    daughter,
  And do not tremble so;
For I can weather the roughest gale,
  That ever wind did blow."

He wrapped her warm in his
    seaman's coat,
  Against the stinging blast;
He cut a rope from a broken spar
  And bound her to the mast.

"O father! I hear the church-bells
    ring,
  O say, what may it be?"
"'Tis a fog-bell on a rock-bound
    coast!" —
  And he steered for the open sea.

"O father! I hear the sound of guns,
  O say, what may it be?"
"Some ship in distress, that cannot
    live
  In such an angry sea!"

"O father! I see a gleaming light,
  O say, what may it be?"
But the father answered never a
    word,
  A frozen corpse was he.

Lashed to the helm, all stiff and
    stark,
  With his face turned to the skies,
The lantern gleamed through the
    gleaming snow
  On his fixed and glassy eyes.

Then the maiden clasped her hands
    and prayed
  That saved she might be;
And she thought of Christ, who
    stilled the waves,
  On the Lake of Galilee.

And fast through the midnight dark
    and drear,
  Through the whistling sleet and
    snow,
Like a sheeted ghost, the vessel
    swept
  Towards the reef of Norman's
    Woe.

And ever the fitful gusts between
  A sound came from the land;
It was the sound of the trampling
    surf,
  On the rocks and the hard
    sea-sand.

The breakers were right beneath her
    bows,
  She drifted a dreary wreck,
And a whooping billow swept the
    crew
  Like icicles from her deck.

She struck where the white and
    fleecy waves
  Looked soft as carded wool,
But the cruel rocks, they gored her
    side
  Like the horns of an angry bull.

Her rattling shrouds, all sheathed in
    ice,
  With the masts went by the board;
Like a vessel of glass, she stove and
    sank,
  Ho! ho! the breakers roared!

At daybreak, on the bleak
    sea beach,
  A fisherman stood aghast,
To see the form of a maiden fair,
  Lashed close to a drifting mast.

The salt sea was frozen on her breast,
  The salt tears in her eyes;
And he saw her hair, like the brown
    seaweed,
  On the billows fall and rise.

Such was the wreck of the Hesperus,
  In the midnight and the snow!
Christ save us all from a death like
    this,
  On the reef of Norman's Woe!

Henry Wadsworth Longfellow

Grandpa Dropped His Glasses

Grandpa dropped his glasses once
In a pot of dye,
And when he put them on again
He saw a purple sky.
Purple fires were rising up
From a purple hill,
Men were grinding purple cider
At a purple mill.
Purple Adeline was playing
With a purple doll;
Little purple dragonflies
Were crawling up the wall.
And at the supper-table
He got a crazy loon
From eating purple apple dumplings
With a purple spoon.

Leroy F. Jackson

The Little Turtle

There was a little turtle,
He lived in a box,
He swam in a puddle,
He climbed on the rocks.

He snapped at a mosquito.
He snapped at a flea.
He snapped at a minnow,
And he snapped at me.

He caught the mosquito.
He caught the flea.
He caught the minnow,
But he didn't catch me.

Vachel Lindsay

The Leak in the Dike

The good dame looked from her
    cottage
    At the close of the pleasant day,
And cheerily called to her little son
    Outside the door at play:
"Come, Peter! Come! I want you to
    go,
    While there is light to see,
To the hut of the blind old man who
    lives
    Across the dike, for me;
And take these cakes I made for
    him —
    They are hot and smoking yet;
You have time enough to go and
    come
    Before the sun is set."

Then the good wife turned to her
    labor,
    Humming a simple song,
And thought of her husband
    working hard
    At the sluices all day long;
And set the turf a-blazing,
    And brought the coarse black
    bread:
That he might find a fire at night,
    And find the table spread.

And Peter left the brother,
    With whom all day he had played,
And the sister who had watched
    their sports
    In the willow's tender shade;
And told them they'd see him back
    before
    They saw a star in sight,
Though he wouldn't be afraid to go
    In the very darkest night!
For he was a brave, bright fellow,
    With eye and conscience clear;
He could do whatever a boy might
    do,
    And he had not learned to fear.
Why, he wouldn't have robbed a
    bird's nest
    Nor brought a stork to harm,
Though never a law in Holland
    Had stood to stay his arm!

And now with his face all glowing,
  And eyes as bright as the day
With the thoughts of his pleasant
    errand,
  He trudged along the way;
And soon his joyous prattle
  Made glad a lonesome place —
Alas! if only the blind old man
  Could have seen that happy face!
Yet he somehow caught the
    brightness
  Which his voice and presence lent
And he felt the sunshine come and
    go
  As Peter came and went.

And now, as the day was sinking,
  And the winds began to rise,
The mother looked from her door
    again,
  Shading her anxious eyes,
And saw the shadows deepen
  And birds to their home come
    back,
But never a sign of Peter
  Along the level track.
But she said: "He will come at
    morning,
  So I need not fret or grieve —
Though it isn't like my boy at all
  To stay without my leave."

But where was the child delaying?
  On the homeward way was he,
And across the dike while the sun
    was up
  An hour above the sea.
He was stopping to gather flowers,
  Now listening to the sound,
As the angry waters dashed
    themselves
  Against their narrow bound.
"Ah! well for us," said Peter,
  "That the gates are good and
    strong,
And my father tends them carefully,
  Or they would not hold you long!
You're a wicked sea," said Peter;
  "I know why you fret and chafe;
You would like to spoil our lands
    and homes;

But our sluices keep you safe."
But hark! through the noise
    of waters
Comes a low, clear, trickling
    sound;
And the child's face pales with
    terror,
  And his blossoms drop to the
    ground.
He is up the bank in a moment,
  And, stealing through the sand,
He sees a stream not yet so large
  As his slender, childish hand.

"Tis a leak in the dike!" — He is but a
    boy,
  Unused to fearful scenes;
But, young as he is, he has learned to
    know
  The dreadful thing that means.
"A leak in the dike!" The stoutest
    heart
  Grows faint that cry to hear,
And the bravest man in all the land
  Turns white with mortal fear.
For he knows the smallest leak may
    grow
  To a flood in a single night;
And he knows the strength of the
    cruel sea
  When loosed in its angry might.

And the boy! He has seen the danger
  And, shouting a wild alarm,
He forces back the weight of the sea
  With the strength of his single
    arm!
He listens for the joyful sound
  Of a footstep passing nigh;
And lays his ear to the ground to
    catch
  The answers to his cry.
And he hears the rough winds
    blowing,
  And the waters rise and fall,
But never an answer comes to him
  Save the echo of his call.
He sees no hope, no succor,
  His feeble voice is lost;
Yet what shall he do but watch and
    wait
  Though he perish at his post!

So, faintly calling and crying
  Till the sun is under the sea;
Crying and moaning till the stars
  Come out for company;
He thinks of his brother and sister,
  Asleep in their safe warm bed;
He thinks of his father and mother,
  Of himself as dying — and dead;
And of how, when the night is over,
  They must come and find him at
    last;
But he never thinks he can leave the
    place
  Where duty holds him fast.

The good dame in the cottage
  Is up and astir with the light,
For the thought of her little Peter
  Has been with her all the night.
And now she watches the pathway,
  As yester-eve she had done;
But what does she see so strange and
    black
  Against the rising sun?
Her neighbors are bearing between
    them
  Something straight to her door;
Her child is coming home, but not
  As he ever came before!

"He is dead!" she cries. "My
    darling!"
  And the startled father hears,
And comes and looks the way she
    looks,
  And fears the thing she fears;
Till a glad shout from the bearers
  Thrills the stricken man and
      wife —
"Give thanks, for your son has saved
    our land,
  And God has saved his life!"
So there in the morning sunshine
  They knelt about the boy;
And every head was bared and bent
  In tearful, reverent joy.

'Tis many a year since then; but still
  When the sea roars like a flood,
The boys are taught what a boy can
    do
  Who is brave and true and good;
For every man in that country
  Takes his son by the hand
And tells him of little Peter,
  Whose courage saved the land.
They may have a valiant hero,
  Remembered through the years;
But never one whose name so oft
  Is named with loving tears.
And his deed shall be sung by the
    cradle,
  And told to the child on the knee,
So long as the dikes of Holland
  Divide the land from the sea!

Phoebe Cary.

The Travelers

The moon and the satellite orbit
   together,
Tracing trackless circles in an end-
   less sky,
The satellite turns to the moon in
   wonder
As they sail over continent, ocean,
   and sea,
Muses over Africa, Afghanistan,
   Alaska,
"Can it be that I'll become ancient as
   she?"
Sailing South America the moon
   looks backward,
Skims the towering Andes with
   scarcely a sigh,
  "Wait, wait,
  Wait," she whispers,
  "Time is nothing
  In the endless sky."

Patricia Hubbell

A Kite

I often sit and wish that I
Could be a kite up in the sky,
And ride upon the breeze and go
Whichever way I chanced to blow.
Then I could look beyond the town,
And see the river winding down,
And follow all the ships that sail
Like me before the merry gale,
Until at last with them I came
To some place with a foreign name.

Frank Dempster Sherman

The Nightingale and the Glowworm

A nightingale that all day long
Had cheer'd the village with his
   song,
Nor yet at eve his note suspended,
Nor yet when eventide was ended,
Began to feel, as well he might,
The keen demands of appetite;
When looking early around,
He spied far off, upon the ground,
A something shining in the dark,
And knew the Glowworm by his
   spark;
So, stooping down from hawthorn
   top,
He thought to put him in his crop.
The worm, aware of his intent,
Harangued him thus, right
   eloquent —:
"Did you admire my lamp," quoth
   he,
"As much as I your minstrelsy,
You would abhor to do me wrong,
As much as I to spoil your song:
For 'twas the self-same Power
   Divine
Taught you to sing, and me to shine;
That you with music, I with light,
Might beautify and cheer the night."
The songster heard this short
   oration,
And warbling out his approbation,
Released him, as my story tells,
And found a supper somewhere
   else.

William Cowper

I Meant to Do My Work Today

I meant to do my work today,
But a brown bird sang in the apple-
        tree,
And a butterfly flitted across the
        field,
And all the leaves were calling me.

And the wind went sighing over the
        land,
Tossing the grasses to and fro,
And a rainbow held out its shining
        hand —
So what could I do but laugh and go?

Richard Le Gallienne

When You and I Grow Up

When you and I
Grow up — Polly —
    I mean that you and me
Shall go sailing in a big ship
    Right over all the sea.
We'll wait till we are older,
    For if we went today,
You know that we might lose
        ourselves,
    And never find the way.

Kate Greenaway

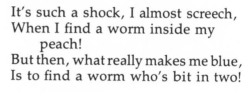

It's such a shock, I almost screech,
When I find a worm inside my
        peach!
But then, what really makes me blue,
Is to find a worm who's bit in two!

William Cole

The Mountain and the Squirrel

The mountain and the squirrel
Had a quarrel,
And the former called the latter
    "Little prig":
Bun replied,
"You are doubtless very big;
But all sorts of things and weather
Must be taken in together
To make up a year,
And a sphere.
And I think it no disgrace
To occupy my place.
If I'm not so large as you,
You are not so small as I,
And not half so spry.
I'll not deny you make
A very pretty squirrel track.
Talents differ; all is well and wisely
        put,
If I cannot carry forests on my back,
Neither can you crack a nut."

Ralph Waldo Emerson

Algy Met a Bear

Algy met a bear,
The bear was bulgy,
The bulge was Algy.

The Skeleton in Armor

"Speak! speak! thou fearful guest!
Who, with thy hollow breast
Still in rude armor drest,
   Comest to daunt me!
Wrapt not in Eastern balms,
But with thy fleshless palms
Stretched, as if asking alms,
   Why does thou haunt me?''

Then, from those cavernous eyes
Pale flashes seemed to rise,
As when the Northern skies
   Gleam in December;
And, like the water's flow
Under December's snow,
Came a dull voice of woe
   From the heart's chamber.

"I was a Viking old!
My deeds, though manifold,
No Skald in song has told
   No Saga taught thee!
Take heed, that in thy verse
Thou dost the tale rehearse,
Else dread a dead man's curse;
   For this I sought thee.

"Far in the Northern Land,
By the wild Baltic's strand,
I, with my childish hand,
   Tames the ger-falcon;
And, with my skates fast-bound,
Skimmed the half-frozen Sound,
That the poor whimpering hound
   Trembled to walk on.

"Oft to his frozen lair
Tracked I the grisly bear,
While from my path the hare
   Fled like a shadow;
Oft through the forest dark
Followed the were-wolf's bark,
Until the soaring lark
   Sang from the meadow.

"But when I older grew,
Joining a corsair's crew,
O'er the dark sea I flew
   With the marauders.
Wild was the life we led;
Many the souls that sped,
Many the hearts that bled,
   By our stern orders.

"Many a wassil-bout
Wore the long Winter out;
Often our midnight shout
   Set the cocks crowing,
As we the Berserk's tale
Measured in cups of ale,
Draining the oaken pail,
   Filled to o'erflowing.

"Once as I told in glee
Tales of the stormy sea,
Soft eyes did gaze on me,
   Burning yet tender;
And as the white stars shine
On the dark Norway pine,
On that dark heart of mine
   Fell their soft splendor.

"I wooed the blue-eyed maid,
Yielding, yet half afraid,
And in the forest's shade
   Our vows were plighted.
Under its loosened vest
Fluttered her little breast,
Like birds within their nest
   By the hawk frighted.

"Bright in her father's hall
Shields gleamed upon the wall,
Loud sang the minstrels all,
   Chanting his glory;
When of old Hildebrand
I asked his daughter's hand,
Mute did the minstrels stand
   To hear my story.

"While the brown ale he quaffed,
Loud then the champion laughed,
And as the wind-gusts waft
   The sea-foam brightly,
So the loud laugh of scorn,
Out of those lips unshorn,
From the deep drinking horn
   Blew the foam lightly.

"She was a Prince's child,
I but a Viking wild,
And though she blushed and
   smiled,
   I was discarded!
Should not the dove so white
Follow the sea-mew's flight,
Why did they leave that night
   Her nest unguarded?

"Scarce had I put to sea,
Bearing the maid with me,
Fairest of all was she
    Among the Norsemen!
When on the white sea-strand,
Waving his armed hand,
Saw we old Hildebrand,
    With twenty horsemen.

"Then launched they to the blast,
Bent like a reed each mast,
Yet we were gaining fast,
    When the wind failed us;
And with a sudden flaw
Came round the gusty Skaw,
So that our foe we saw
    Laugh as he failed us.

"And as to catch the gale
Round veered the flapping sail,
Death! was the helmsman's hail,
    Death without quarter!
Mid-ships with iron keel
Struck we her ribs of steel;
Down her black hulk did reel
    Through the black water!

"As with his wings aslant,
Sails the fierce cormorant,
Seeking some rocky haunt,
    With his prey laden,
So toward the open main,
Beating to sea again,
Through the wild hurricane,
    Bore I the maiden.

"Three weeks we westward bore,
And when the storm was o'er,
Cloud-like we saw the shore
    Stretching to leeward;
There for my lady's bower
    Built I the lofty tower,
Which, to this very hour,
    Stands looking sea-ward.

"There lived we many years;
Time dried the maiden's tears;
She had forgot her fears,
    She was a mother;
Death closed her mild blue eyes,
Under that tower she lies!
Ne'er shall the sun arise
    On such another!

"Still grew my bosom then,
Still as a stagnant fen!
Hateful to me were men,
    The sunlight hateful!
In the vast forest here,
Clad in my warlike gear,
Fell I upon my spear,
    O, death was grateful!

"Thus, seamed with many scars,
Bursting these prisons bars,
Up to its native stars
    My soul ascended!
There from the flowing bowl
Deep drinks the warrior's soul,
Skoal! to the Northland! *Skoal!*"
    — Thus the tale ended.

Henry Wadsworth Longfellow

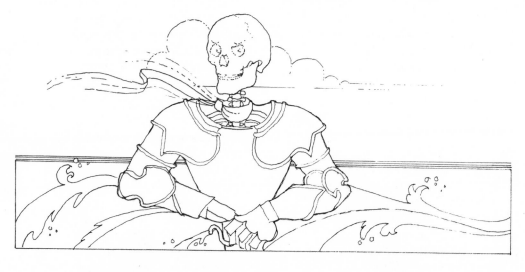

Around the Year

Snowy, Flowy, Blowy,
Showery, Flowery, Bowery,
Hoppy, Croppy, Droppy,
Breezy, Sneezy, Freezy.

(The Twelve Months)
Sir Gregory Gander
[George Ellis]

Thirty days hath September,
April, June, and November;
All the rest have thirty-one;
Except February alone,
Which has four and twenty-four
And every fourth year, one day
     more.

Nursery Rhyme

The New Year

Farewell old year,
With goodness crowned,
A hand divine hath set thy bound.

Welcome New Year,
Which shall bring
Fresh blessings from
Our Lord and King.

The old we leave without a tear,
The new we enter without fear.

Spring is showery, flowery, bowery;
Summer: hoppy, croppy, poppy;
Autumn: wheezy, sneezy, freezy;
Winter: slippy, drippy, nippy.

Mother Goose

Thirty days hath September,
April, June, and November,
Save February; the rest have thirty-
    one
Unless you hear from Washington.

To My Valentine

If apples were pears,
And peaches were plums,
And the rose had a different name;
If tigers were bears,
And fingers were thumbs,
I'd love you just the same!

For, lo, the winter is past,
The rain is over and gone;
The flowers appear on the earth;
The time of the singing of birds is
    come,
And the voice of the turtle is heard in
    our land.

The Bible, Song of Solomon 2:11,12

Tomorrow is Saint Valentine's Day,
    All in the morning betime,
And I a maid at your window,
    To be your Valentine.

William Shakespeare

Written in March

The cock is crowing,
The stream is flowing,
The small birds twitter,
The lake doth glitter,
The green field sleeps in the sun;
The oldest and youngest
Are at work with the strongest;
The cattle are grazing,
Their heads never raising;
There are forty feeding like one!

Like an army defeated
The snow hath retreated,
And now doth fare ill
On the top of the bare hill;
The ploughboy is whooping —
    anon-anon:
There's joy in the mountains;
There's life in the fountains;
Small clouds are sailing,
Blue sky prevailing;
The rain is over and gone!

William Wordsworth

God's Plan for Spring

It never has failed, and it never will,
The wind swings around and the
    violets come;
There's a touch of green on a bare
    gray hill,
And the robin is building himself a
    home.

Year after year, year after year —
That is the way that God has
    planned —
We feel a loveliness somewhere
    near,
And spring comes moving across
    the land.

Boughs grow heavy with leaf and
    bud,
The sky is a sea with drifting sails;
And spring comes back, as we knew
    she would,
That is God's plan, and it never fails.

Nancy Byrd Turner

On Easter Day

Easter lilies! Can you hear
What they whisper, low and clear?
In dewy fragrance they unfold
Their splendor sweet, their snow
    and gold.
Every beauty-breathing bell
News of heaven has to tell.
Listen to their mystic voice,
Hear, oh mortal, and rejoice!
Hark, their soft and heavenly chime!
Christ is risen for all time!

Celia Laighton Thaxter

In the bonds of Death He lay
    Who for our offense was slain;
But the Lord is risen to-day,
    Christ hath brought us life again,
Wherefore let us all rejoice,
Singing loud, with cheerful voice,
    Hallelujah!

Martin Luther

We have tulips in our flower bed.
This spring they looked so pretty —
    pink and white.
Now they've gone to sleep in small
    brown bulbs.
Next spring they'll bloom again —
    still pink and white.
All winter God remembers who they
    are,
And never gets them mixed with
    other things.
I'm sure he'll always know that I am
    me.

Jessie Orton Jones
(VII from Secrets)

I am the resurrection, and the life:
he that believeth in me, though he
        were dead, yet shall he live:
And whosoever liveth and believeth
    in me shall never die.
Believest thou this?

The Bible, John 11:25,26

Wise Johnny

Little Johnny-jump-up said,
"It must be spring,
I just saw a lady-bug
And heard a robin sing."

Edwina Fallis

23

April Fool's Day

The first of April, some do say,
Is set apart for All Fools' Day,
But why the people call it so,
Nor I, nor they themselves, do
    know.

Old English Almanac

May Day

Spring is coming, spring is coming,
    Birdies, build your nest;
Weave together straw and feather,
    Doing each your best.

Spring is coming, spring is coming,
    Flowers are coming too:
Pansies, lilies, daffodillies,
    Now are coming through.

Spring is coming, spring is coming,
    All around is fair;
Shimmer and quiver on the river,
    Joy is everywhere.
We wish you a happy May.

Remembering Day

All the soldiers marching along;
All the children singing a song;
All the flowers dewy and sweet;
All the flags hung out in the street;
Hearts that throb in a grateful way —
For this is our Remembering Day.*

Mary Wright Saunders

*Memorial Day

A Day in June

And what is so rare as a day in June?
    Then, if ever, come perfect days;
Then Heaven tries earth if it be in
    tune,
    And over it softly her warm ear
    lays;
Whether we look, or whether we
    listen,
    We hear life murmur, or see it
    glisten;
Every clod feels a stir of might,
    An instinct within it that reaches
    and towers,
And, groping blindly above it for
    light,
    Climbs to a soul in grass and
    flowers.

James Russell Lowell
(from The Vision of Sir Launfal)

Fourth of July

Fat torpedoes in bursting jackets,
Firecrackers in scarlet packets.
We'll be up at crack o' day,
Fourth of July — Hurrah! Hooray!

Rachel Field

The Fourth of July

Day of glory! Welcome day!
Freedom's banners greet thy ray;
See! how cheerfully they play
    With thy morning breeze,
On the rocks where pilgrims
    kneeled,
On the heights where squadrons
    wheeled,
When a tyrant's thunder pealed
    O'er the trembling seas.

God of armies! did thy stars
On their courses smite his oars,
Blast his arm, and wrest his bars
   From the heaving tide?
On our standard, lo! they burn,
And, when days like this return,
Sparkle o'er the soldier's urn
   Who for freedom died.

God of peace! whose spirit fills
All the echoes of our hills,
All the murmur of our rills,
   Now the storm is o'er,
O let free men be our sons,
And let future Washingtons
Rise to lead their valiant ones
   Till there's war no more!

John Pierpont

Benjamin Jones Goes Swimming

Benjamin Jones in confident tones
   Told his wife, "On the Fourth of
      July
I think I'll compete in the free-for-all
   meet,
   I bet I can win, if I try."

But his wife said, "My word! How
   very absurd!
   You haven't gone swimming for
     years.
With others so fast, you're sure to be
   LAST,
   And I'll blush to the tips of my
     ears."

Well, the Fourth quickly came, and
   waiting acclaim
   Were wonderful swimmers
     galore,
Each poised in his place for the start
   of the race,
   While spectators crowded the
     shore.

The contest began, and Benjy, poor
   man,
   Was passed on the left and the
     right.
His pace was so slow that a crab saw
   his toe
   And thought it would venture a
     bite.

Ben noticed the crab as it started to
   grab
   And — perhaps the result can be
     guessed;
The thought of his toe in the claws of
   his foe
   Made him swim like a swimmer
     possessed!

And the crowd on the shore sent up a
   great roar
   As Ben took the lead in the dash,
While his wife on the dock received
   such a shock
   She fell in the lake with a splash.

Aileen Fisher

August

Buttercup nodded and said
   good-by,
   Clover and daisy went off
     together,
But the fragrant water lilies lie
   Yet moored in the golden August
     weather.
The swallows chatter about their
   flight,
   The cricket chirps like a rare good
     fellow,
The asters twinkle in clusters bright,
   While the corn grows ripe and the
     apples mellow.

Celia Laighton Thaxter

The Mist and All

I like the fall,
The mist and all.
I like the night owl's
Lonely call —
And wailing sound
Of wind around.

I like the gray
November day,
And bare, dead boughs
That coldly sway
Against my pane.
I like the rain.

I like to sit
And laugh at it —
And tend
My cozy fire a bit.
I like the fall —
The mist and all.

Dixie Willson

Summer Days

Winter is cold-hearted;
   Spring is yea and nay;
Autumn is a weathercock,
   Blown every way:
Summer days for me,
When every leaf is on its tree,

When Robin's not a beggar,
   And Jenny Wren's a bride,
And larks hang, singing, singing,
    singing,
   Over the wheat-fields wide,
   And anchored lilies ride,
And the pendulum spider
   Swings from side to side,

And blue-black beetles transact
    business,
   And gnats fly in a host,
And furry caterpillars hasten
   That no time be lost,
And moths grow fat and thrive,
And ladybirds arrive.

Before green apples blush,
   Before green nuts embrown,
Why, one day in the country
   Is worth a month in town —
Is worth a day and a year
   Of the dusty, musty, lag-last
    fashion
That days drone elsewhere.

Christina Rossetti

Black and Gold

Everything is black and gold,
   Black and gold, tonight;
Yellow pumpkins, yellow moon,
   Yellow candlelight.

Jet-black cat with golden eyes,
   Shadows black as ink,
Firelight blinking in the dark
   With a yellow blink.

Black and gold, black and gold,
  Nothing in between —
When the world turns black and
    gold,
  Then it's Halloween!

Nancy Byrd Turner

Something Told the Wild Geese

Something told the wild geese
  It was time to go.
Though the fields lay golden,
  Something whispered — "Snow."
Leaves were green and stirring,
  Berries, luster-glossed,
But beneath warm feathers,
  Something cautioned — "Frost."
All the sagging orchards
  Steamed with amber spice,
But each wild breast stiffened
  At remembered ice.
Something told the wild geese
  It was time to fly —
Summer sun was on their wings,
  Winter in their cry.

Rachel Field

Thanksgiving

I thank you, God,
That swallows know their way
In the great sky;
That grass, all brown today,
And dead and dry,
Will quiver in the sun
All green and gay
When winter's done.

Louise Driscoll

Thanksgiving Day

Over the river and through the
    wood,
  To grandfather's house we'll go;
    The horse knows the way
    To carry the sleigh,
  Through the white and drifted
    snow.

Over the river and through the
    wood —
  Oh, how the wind does blow!
    It stings the toes
    And bites the nose,
  As over the ground we go.

Over the river and through the
    wood,
  To have a first-rate play.
    Hear the bells ring!
    "Ting-ling-ding!"
  Hurrah for Thanksgiving Day!

Over the river and through the
    wood,
  Trot fast, my dapple-gray!
    Spring over the ground,
    Like a hunting-hound:
  For this is Thanksgiving Day.

Over the river and through the
    wood,
  And straight through the
      barnyard gate.
    We seem to go
    Extremely slow —
  It is so hard to wait!

Over the river and through the
    wood,
  Now grandmother's cap I spy!
    Hurrah for the fun!
    Is the pudding done?
  Hurrah for the pumpkin pie!

Lydia Maria Child

November

No sun — no moon!
No morn — no noon —
No dawn — no dusk — no proper
    time of day —
No sky — no earthly view —
No distance looking blue —
No road — no street — no "t'other
    side the way" —
No end to any row —
No indications where the crescents
    go —
No top to any steeple —
No recognitions of familiar
    people —
No courtesies for showing 'em —
No knowing 'em!
No traveling at all — no
    locomotion —
No inkling of the way — no notion
"No go" — by land or ocean —
No mail — no post —
No news from any foreign coast —
No park — no ring — no afternoon
    gentility —
No company — no nobility —
No warmth, no cheerfulness, no
    healthful ease,
No comfortable feel in any
    member —
No shade, no shine, no butterflies,
    no bees,
No fruits, no flowers, no leaves, no
    birds —
November!

Thomas Hood

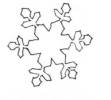

Snow-Stars

The air is full of flying stars,
    The sky is shaking down
A million silver stars of snow
    On wood and field and town.

Frances Frost

Come, Ye Thankful People

Come, ye thankful people, come
Raise the song of harvest home;
    All is safely gathered in,
    Ere the winter storms begin;
God our Maker doth provide
For our wants to be supplied;
    Come to God's own temple, come,
    Raise the song of harvest home.

All the world is God's own field
Fruit unto his praise to yield;
    Wheat and tares together sown,
    Unto joy or sorrow grown;
First the blade, and then the ear,
Then the full corn shall appear;
    Lord of harvest, grant that we
    Wholesome grain and pure may
    be.

Henry Alford

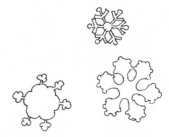

Falling Snow

See the pretty snowflakes
    Falling from the sky;
On the walk and housetop
    Soft and thick they lie.

On the window-ledges
    On the branches bare;
Now how fast they gather,
    Filling all the air.

Look into the garden,
    Where the grass was green;
Covered by the snowflakes,
    Not a blade is seen.

Now the bare black bushes
    All look soft and white,
Every twig is laden —
    What a pretty sight!

There were some shepherds living in the same part of the country, keeping guard throughout the night over their flock in the open fields. Suddenly an angel of the Lord stood before them, the splendour of the Lord blazed around them, and they were terror-stricken. But the angel said to them,

"Do not be afraid! Listen, I bring you glorious news of great joy which is for all the people. This very day, in David's town, a Saviour has been born for you. He is Christ, the Lord. Let this prove it to you: you will find a baby, wrapped up and lying in a manger."

And in a flash there appeared with the angel a vast host of the armies of Heaven, praising God, saying,

"Glory to God in the highest Heaven! Peace upon earth among men of goodwill!"

When the angels left them and went back into Heaven, the shepherds said to each other,

"Now let us go straight to Bethlehem and see this thing which the Lord has made known to us."

So they went as fast as they could and they found Mary and Joseph — and the baby lying in the manger. And when they had seen this sight, they told everybody what had been said to them about the little child. And all those who heard them were amazed at what the shepherds said. But Mary treasured all these things and turned them over in her mind. The shepherds went back to work, glorifying and praising God for everything that they had heard and seen, which had happened just as they had been told.

The Bible, Luke 2:8-20, Phillips

Long, Long Ago

Winds through the olive trees
  Softly did blow,
Round little Bethlehem,
  Long, long ago.

Sheep on the hillside lay
  Whiter than snow;
Shepherds were watching them,
  Long, long ago.

Then from the happy skies,
  Angels bent low,
Singing their songs of joy,
  Long, long ago.

For in a manger bed,
  Cradled we know,
Christ came to Bethlehem,
  Long, long ago.

Katherine Parker

Cradle Hymn

Away in a manger,
  No crib for a bed,
The little Lord Jesus
  Lay down his sweet head;
The stars in the heavens
  Looked down where he lay,
The little Lord Jesus
  Asleep in the hay.

The cattle are lowing,
  The poor baby wakes,
But little Lord Jesus
  No crying he makes.
I love thee, Lord Jesus,
  Look down from the sky,
And stay by my cradle
  Till morning is nigh.

Martin Luther

I Heard the Bells on Christmas Day

I heard the bells on Christmas day
Their old familiar carols play,
And wild and sweet the words
    repeat
Of peace on earth, good-will to men.

I thought how, as the day had come,
The belfries of all Christendom
Had rolled along the unbroken song
Of peace on earth, good-will to men.

And in despair I bowed my head:
"There is no peace on earth," I said:
"For hate is strong and mocks the
    song
Of peace on earth, good-will to
    men."

Then pealed the bells more loud and
    deep:
"God is not dead, no doth he sleep:
The wrong shall fail, the right
    prevail,
With peace on earth, good-will to
    men."

Till ringing, singing on its way
The world revolved from night to
    day,
A voice, a chime, a chant sublime,
Of peace on earth, good-will to men.

Henry Wadsworth Longfellow

Song

Why do bells for Christmas ring?
Why do little children sing?

Once a lovely, shining star,
Seen by shepherds from afar,
Gently moved until its light
Made a manger's cradle bright.

There a darling baby lay,
Pillowed soft upon the hay;
And its mother sang and smiled,
"This is Christ, the holy child!"

Therefore bells for Christmas ring,
Therefore little children sing.

Eugene Field

The Christmas Exchange

When Bill gives me a book, I know
It's just the book he wanted, so
When I give him a Ping-Pong set,
He's sure it's what I hoped to get.

Then after Christmas we arrange
A little Christmas gift exchange;
I give the book to him, and he
Gives back the Ping-Pong set to me.

So each gives twice — and that is
    pleasant —
To get the truly wanted present.

Arthur Guiterman

Christmas Everywhere

Everywhere, everywhere, Christmas
    to-night!
Christmas in lands of the fir-tree and
    pine,
Christmas in lands of the palm-tree
    and vine,
Christmas where snow-peaks stand
    solemn and white,
Christmas where cornfields lie
    sunny and bright,
    Everywhere, everywhere,
        Christmas to-night!

Christmas where children are
    hopeful and gay,
Christmas where old men are
    patient and gray,
Christmas where peace, like a dove
    in its flight,
Broods o'er brave men in the thick of
    the fight.
    Everywhere, everywhere,
        Christmas to-night!

For the Christ-child who comes is
    the Master of all,
No palace too great and no cottage
    too small;

The angels who welcome Him sing
    from the height,
"In the City of David, a King in His
    might."
    Everywhere, everywhere,
        Christmas to-night!

Then let every heart keep its
    Christmas within,
Christ's pity for sorrow, Christ's
    hatred for sin,
Christ's care for the weakest,
    Christ's courage for right,
Christ's dread of the darkness,
    Christ's love of the light,
    Everywhere, everywhere,
        Christmas to-night!

So the stars of the midnight which
    compass us round
Shall see a strange glory and hear a
    sweet sound,
And cry, "Look! the earth is aflame
    with delight,
O sons of the morning, rejoice at the
    sight."
    Everywhere, everywhere,
        Christmas to-night!

Phillips Brooks

Christmas Carol

God bless the master of this house,
    The mistress also,
And all the little children,
    That round the table go,
And all your kin and kinsmen
    That dwell both far and near;
I wish you a Merry Christmas
    And a Happy New Year.

A Visit from St. Nicholas

'Twas the night before Christmas,
    when all through the house
Not a creature was stirring, not even
    a mouse;
The stockings were hung by the
    chimney with care,
In hopes that St. Nicholas soon
    would be there;
The children were nestled all snug in
    their beds
While visions of sugar-plums
    danced in their heads;
And mamma in her kerchief, and I in
    my cap,
Had just settled our brains for a long
    winter's nap, —
When out on the lawn there arose
    such a clatter,
I sprang from my bed to see what
    was the matter.
Away to the window I flew like a
    flash,
Tore open the shutters and threw up
    the sash.
The moon on the breast of the new-
    fallen snow
Gave a lustre of midday to objects
    below;
When what to my wondering eyes
    should appear,

But a miniature sleigh and eight tiny
    reindeer,
With a little old driver, so lively and
    quick,
I knew in a moment it must be St.
    Nick.
More rapid than eagles his coursers
    they came,
And he whistled and shouted, and
    called them by name:
"Now, Dasher! now, Dancer! now,
    Prancer and Vixen!
On, Comet! on, Cupid! on, Donder
    and Blitzen!
To the top of the porch, to the top of
    the wall!
Now dash away, dash away, dash
    away, all!"
As dry leaves that before the wild
    hurricane fly,
When they meet with an obstacle,
    mount to the sky,
So up to the housetop the coursers
    they flew,
With the sleigh full of toys, and St.
    Nicholas too.
And then in a twinkling I heard on
    the roof
The prancing and pawing of each
    little hoof.
As I drew in my head, and was
    turning around,

Down the chimney St. Nicholas
    came with a bound.
He was dressed all in fur from his
    head to his foot,
And his clothes were all tarnished
    with ashes and soot;
A bundle of toys he had flung on his
    back,
And he looked like a peddler just
    opening his pack.
His eyes — how they twinkled! his
    dimples, how merry!
His cheeks were like roses, his nose
    like a cherry!
His droll little mouth was drawn up
    like a bow,
And the beard on his chin was as
    white as the snow.
The stump of a pipe he held tight in
    his teeth,
And the smoke it encircled his head
    like a wreath.
He had a broad face and a little
    round belly
That shook, when he laughed, like a
    bowl full of jelly.
He was chubby and plump, a right
    jolly old elf;
And I laughed when I saw him, in
    spite of myself.
A wink of his eye and a twist of his
    head
Soon gave me to know I had nothing
    to dread.
He spoke not a word, but went
    straight to his work,
And filled all the stockings; then
    turned with a jerk,
And laying his finger aside of his
    nose,
And giving a nod, up the chimney
    he rose.
He sprang to his sleigh, to his team
    gave a whistle,
And away they all flew like the down
    of a thistle;
But I heard him exclaim, ere he
    drove out of sight,
"Happy Christmas to all, and to all a
    good-night!"

Clement C. Moore

Mister Snow Man

A cranberry nose and a tin-can hat
Belong to a snow man, jolly and fat.
We rolled him up by the fence today.
Please, Mr. Sun, don't melt him
    away!

Bertha Wilcox Smith

Around the Year

January brings the snow,
    Makes our feet and fingers glow,
February brings the rain,
    Thaws the frozen lake again,
March brings breezes loud and
    shrill,
    Stirs the dancing daffodil.

April brings the primrose sweet,
    Scatters daisies at our feet,
May brings flocks of pretty lambs,
    Skipping by their fleecy dams,
June brings tulips, lilies, roses,
    Fills the children's hands with
    posies.

Hot July brings cooling showers,
    Apricots and gillyflowers,
August brings the sheaves of corn,
    Then the harvest home is borne.
Warm September brings the fruit,
    Sportsmen then begin to shoot.

Fresh October brings the pheasant,
    Then to gather nuts is pleasant,
Dull November brings the blast,
    Then the leaves are whirling fast.
Chill December brings the sleet,
    Blazing fire and Christmas treat.

Sara Coleridge

Beauty and Discovery

It is not raining rain to me,
    It's raining daffodils;
In every dimpled drop I see
    Wildflowers on the hills.
The clouds of gray engulf the day,
    And overwhelm the town;
It is not raining rain to me,
    It's raining roses down.

It is not raining rain to me,
    But fields of clover bloom,
Where every buccaneering bee
    May find a bed and room.
A health unto the happy!
    A fig for him who frets!
It is not raining rain to me,
    It's raining violets.

(April Rain)
Robert Loveman

The Rainbow

I saw the lovely arch
Of Rainbow span the sky,
The gold sun burning
As the rain swept by.

In bright-ringed solitude
The showery foliage shone
One lovely moment,
And the Bow was gone.

Walter de la Mare

Rich with a sprinkling of fair
    musk-rose blooms:
And such too is the grandeur of the
    dooms
We have imagined for the mighty
    dead;
All lovely tales that we have heard or
    read:
An endless fountain of immortal
    drink,
Pouring unto us from the heaven's
    brink.

John Keats

A Thing of Beauty

A thing of beauty is a joy for ever:
Its loveliness increases; it will never
Pass into nothingness; but still will
    keep
A bower quiet for us, and a sleep
Full of sweet dreams, and health,
    and quiet breathing.
Therefore, on every morrow, we are
    wreathing
A flowery band to bind us to the
    earth,
Spite of despondence, of the
    inhuman dearth
Of noble natures, of the gloomy
    days,
Of all the unhealthy and o'er-
    darkened ways
Made for our searching: yes, in spite
    of all,
Some shape of beauty moves away
    the pall
From our dark spirits. Such the sun,
    the moon,
Trees old and young, sprouting a
    shady boon
For simple sheep; and such are
    daffodils
With the green world they live in;
    and clear rills
That for themselves a cooling covert
    make
'Gainst the hot season; the
    mid-forest brake,

Music

Let me go where'er I will,
I hear a sky-born music stiil:
It sounds from all things old,
It sounds from all things young;
From all that's fair, from all that's
    foul,
Peals out a cheerful song.
It is not only in the rose,
It is not only in the bird,
Not only where the rainbow glows,
Nor in the song of woman heard,
But in the darkest, meanest things
There always, always something
    sings.
'Tis not in the high stars alone,
Nor in the cups of budding flowers,
Nor in the redbreast's mellow tone,
Nor in the bow that smiles in
    showers,
But in the mud and scum of things
There always, always something
    sings.

Ralph Waldo Emerson

Holy, holy, holy,
is the Lord of hosts:
the whole earth
is full of his glory.

The Bible, Isaiah 6:3

The Waterfall

Tinkle, tinkle!
Listen well!
Like a fairy silver bell
  In the distance ringing,
   Lightly swinging
    In the air;
'Tis the water in the dell
Where the elfin minstrels dwell,
  Falling in a rainbow sprinkle,
  Dropping stars that brightly
    twinkle,
   Bright and fair,
On the darkling pool below,
Making music so;
  'Tis the water elves who play
  On their lutes of spray.
Tinkle, tinkle!
Like a fairy silver bell;
Like a pebble in a shell;
Tinkle, tinkle!
Listen well!

       Frank Dempster Sherman

  I can climb our apple tree,
If I put my feet carefully in the right
    places,
  And pull myself up by my hands.
Then I come to my little seat in the
    arms of the tree.
  I can sit there and see everything.
I can see a measuring worm, light
    green,
  Climbing our apple tree.
  At every step
He has to make his whole body into
    a hump,
While his back feet catch up with his
    front feet.
That is a hard way to climb a tree,
  But it's his way
  And he doesn't seem to mind.

       Jessie Orton Jones
       (IX from Secrets)

What Do We Plant?

What do we plant when we plant the
    tree?
We plant the ship which will cross
    the sea.
We plant the mast to carry the sails;
We plant the planks to withstand the
    gales —
The keel, the keelson, the beam, the
    knee;
We plant the ship when we plant the
    tree.

What do we plant when we plant the
    tree?
We plant the houses for you and me.
We plant the rafters, the shingles,
    the floors,
We plant the studding, the lath, the
    doors,
The beams and siding, all parts that
    be;
We plant the house when we plant
    the tree.

What do we plant when we plant the
    tree?
A thousand things that we daily see;
We plant the spire that out-towers
    the crag,
We plant the staff for our country's
    flag,
We plant the shade, from the hot sun
    free;
We plant all these when we plant the
    tree.

Henry Abbey

God Is Everywhere

There's not a tint that paints the rose
    Or decks the lily fair,
Or marks the humblest flower that
    grows,
    But God has placed it there.

There's not a star whose twinkling
    light
    Illumes the spreading earth;
There's not a cloud, so dark or
    bright,
    But wisdom gave it birth.

There's not a place on earth's vast
    round,
    In ocean's deep or air,
Where love and beauty are not
    found,
    For God is everywhere.

I Never Saw a Moor

I never saw a moor;
I never saw the sea,
Yet know I how the heather looks
And what a billow be.

I never spoke with God
Nor visited in heaven,
Yet certain am I of the spot
As if the checks were given.

Emily Dickinson

Boats sail on the rivers,
    And ships sail on the seas;
But clouds that sail across the sky
    Are prettier far than these.

There are bridges on the rivers,
    As pretty as you please;
But the bow that bridges heaven,
    And overtops the trees,
And builds a road from earth to sky,
    Is prettier far than these.

Christina Rossetti

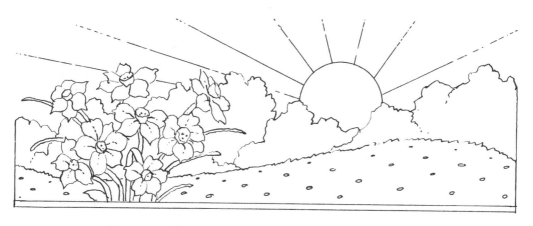

Covering the Subject

The turtle, clam and crab as well
Are covered with a sturdy shell,
While fish, excepting maybe whales,
Are shingled fore and aft with
    scales.

Though most, perhaps, have not the
    plating
Of armadillos, it's worth stating
That animals at least have hides
That give them fairly firm outsides.

And yet that upright mammal, man,
Must get along as best he can
With nothing but a little skin
To keep his precious insides in.

Richard Armour

Flowers always know what they
    should do.
The buttercup grows always shining
    yellow
  And the larkspur blue.
The lily always smells like lily,
  And the rose like rose.
Do you suppose the yellow
    buttercup
  Would like to be a rose?
Or the rose have the perfume of a
    lily?
  I think each one looks happy
  Being its very own self!

Jessie Orton Jones
(VI from Secrets)

Spring Song

The year's at the spring
And day's at the morn;
Morning's at seven;
The hillside's dew-pearled;
The lark's on the wing;
The snail's on the thorn;
God's in his heaven —
All's right with the world!

Robert Browning
(from Pippa Passes)

I Like to See It Lap the Miles

I like to see it lap the miles —
And lick the valleys up —
And stop to feed itself at banks;
And then, prodigious, step

Around a pile of mountains
And, supercilious, peer
In shanties by the sides of roads;
And then a quarry pace,

To fit its sides, and crowd between,
Complaining all the while
In horrid, hooting stanza;
Then chase itself down hill

And neigh like Boanerges —
Then punctual as a star
Stop — docile and omnipotent
At its own stable door.

Emily Dickinson

Leisure

What is this life if, full of care,
We have no time to stand and stare.

No time to stand beneath the boughs
And stare as long as sheep or cows.

No time to see, when woods we
    pass,
Where squirrels hide their nuts in
    grass.

No time to see, in broad daylight,
Streams full of stars, like stars at
    night.

No time to turn at Beauty's glance,
And watch her feet, how they can
    dance.

No time to wait till her mouth can
Enrich that smile her eyes began.

A poor life this if, full of care,
We have no time to stand and stare.

William Henry Davies

Sometimes I hear God's whisper in
    the night.
The birds do, too, because they
    answer him
    In small bird voices.
I think he's telling them just what to
    do.
I think he tells them how to build
    their nests,
    And make them safe for eggs.
He tells them how to feed the baby
    birds.
He tells them when to fly away from
    cold,
And where to find a warmer place to
    live.
    So many things for birds to know!
    So many things to do!

Jessie Orton Jones
(V from Secrets)

The best portion of a good man's
life is his little, nameless, unremem-
bered acts of kindness and of love.

William Wordsworth

Night

My kitten walks on velvet feet
And makes no sound at all;
And in the doorway nightly sits
To watch the darkness fall.

I think he loves the lady, Night,
And feels akin to her
Whose footsteps are as still as his,
Whose touch as soft as fur.

Lois Weakley McKay

If you wisely invest in beauty, it
will remain with you all the days of
your life.

Frank Lloyd Wright

40

The Legend of the Raindrop

The legend of the raindrop
Has a lesson for us all,
As it trembled in the heavens . . .
Questioning whether it should fall
For the glistening raindrop argued
To the genie of the sky,
"I am beautiful and lovely
As I sparkle here on high,
And hanging here I will become
Part of the rainbow's hue
And I'll shimmer like a diamond
For all the world to view." . . .
But the genie told the raindrop,
"Do not hesitate to go,
For you will be more beautiful
If you fall to earth below,
For you will sink into the soil
And be lost a while from sight,
But when you reappear on earth,
You'll be looked on with delight;
For you will be the raindrop
That quenched the thirsty ground
And helped the lovely flowers
To blossom all around,
And in your resurrection
You'll appear in queenly clothes
With the beauty of the lily
And the fragrance of the rose;
Then, when you wilt and wither,
You'll become part of the earth
And make the soil more fertile
And give new flowers birth." . . .
For there is nothing ever lost
Or *eternally neglected*
For *everything God ever made*
Is always resurrected;
So trust God's all-wise wisdom
And doubt the Father never,
For in *His heavenly kingdom*
There is nothing lost forever.

Helen Steiner Rice

She Was a Phantom of Delight

She was a Phantom of delight
When first she gleamed upon my
        sight;
A lovely Apparition, sent
To be a moment's ornament;
Her eyes as stars of Twilight fair;
Like Twilight's, too, her dusky hair;
But all things else about her drawn
From May-time and the cheerful
        Dawn;
A dancing Shape, an Image gay,
To haunt, to startle, and way-lay.

I saw her upon nearer view,
A Spirit, yet a Woman too!
Her household motions light and
        free,
And steps of virgin-liberty;
A countenance in which did meet
Sweet records, promises as sweet;
A Creature not too bright or good
For human nature's daily food;
For transient sorrows, simple wiles,
Praise, blame, love, kisses, tears,
        and smiles.

And now I see with eye serene
The very pulse of the machine;
A Being breathing thoughtful
        breath,
A Traveller between life and death;
The reason firm, the temperate will,
Endurance, foresight, strength, and
        skill;
A perfect Woman, nobly planned,
To warn, to comfort, and command;
And yet a Spirit still, and bright,
With something of angelic light.

William Wordsworth

Bits of Wisdom

Little drops of water,
   Little grains of sand,
Make the mighty ocean
   And the pleasant land.

So the little moments,
   Humble though they be,
Make the mighty ages
   Of eternity.

So our little errors
   Lead the soul away
From the path of virtue,
   Far in sin to stray.

Little deeds of kindness,
   Little words of love,
Help make earth happy
   Like the heaven above.

(Little Things)
Julia Carney

A Wise Old Owl

A wise old owl lived in an oak;
The more he saw the less he spoke;
The less he spoke the more he heard:
Why can't we all be like that bird?

Edward Hersey Richards

Bits of Wisdom

Keep conscience clear,
Then never fear.

From a slip of the foot you may soon
    recover,
But a slip of the tongue you may
    never get over.

Tomorrow I'll reform,
The fool does say.
Today's too late,
The wise did yesterday.

Haste
Makes waste.

Benjamin Franklin

He Who Knows

He who knows not, and knows not
    that he knows not, is a fool.
Shun him.
He who knows not, and knows that
    he knows not, is a child.
Teach him.
He who knows, and knows not that
    he knows, is asleep.
Wake him.
He who knows, and knows that he
    knows, is wise.
Follow him.

From the Persian

One, two, whatever you do,
Start it well and carry it through.

From the Sermon on the Mount

Blessed are the poor in spirit:
For theirs is the kingdom of heaven.

Blessed are they that mourn:
For they shall be comforted.

Blessed are the meek:
For they shall inherit the earth.

Blessed are they which do hunger
    and thirst after righteousness:
For they shall be filled.

Blessed are the merciful:
For they shall obtain mercy.

Blessed are the pure in heart:
For they shall see God.

Blessed are the peacemakers:
For they shall be called the children
    of God.

Blessed are they which are
    persecuted for righteousness'
    sake:
For theirs is the kingdom of heaven.

The Bible, Matthew 5:3-10

Four Things

There be four things which are little
    upon the earth,
but they are exceeding wise:

The ants are a people not strong,
yet they prepare their meat in the
    summer;

The conies are but a feeble folk,
yet make they their houses in the
    rocks;

The locusts have no king,
yet go they forth all of them by
    bands;

The spider taketh hold with her
    hands,
and is in kings' palaces.

The Bible, Proverbs 30:24-28

Overheard in an Orchard

Said the Robin to the Sparrow:
  "I should really like to know
Why these anxious human beings
  Rush about and worry so."

Said the Sparrow to the Robin:
  "Friend, I think that it must be
That they have no heavenly Father
  Such as cares for you and me."

Elizabeth Cheney

Good Advice

  Don't shirk
  Your work
For the sake of a dream;
  A fish
  In the dish
Is worth ten in the stream.

*Adapted from the German by
Louis Untermeyer*

The Best Thing to Give

The best thing to give:
  to your enemy is forgiveness;
  to an opponent, tolerance;
  to a friend, your heart;
  to your child, a good example;
  to a father, deference;
  to your mother, conduct that will
      make her proud of you; ·
  to yourself, respect;
  to all men, charity.

Lord Balfour

Four Things

Four things in any land must dwell,
If it endures and prospers well:
One is manhood true and good;
One is noble womanhood;
One is child life, clean and bright;
And one an altar kept alight.

The Frog

Be kind and tender to the Frog,
And do not call him names,
As "Slimey-skin," or "Pollywog,"
Or likewise "Ugly James,"
Or "Gape-a-grin," or "Toad-gone-
    wrong,"
Or "Billy Bandy-knees";
The frog is justly sensitive
To epithets like these.

No animal will more repay
A treatment kind and fair,
At least so lonely people say
Who keep a frog (and, by the way,
They are extremely rare).

Hilaire Belloc .

Circles

The things to draw with compasses
Are suns and moons and circlesses
And rows of humptydumpasses
Or anything in circuses
Like hippopotamusseses
And hoops and camels' humpasses
And wheels on clowneses busseses
And fat old elephumpasses.

Harry Behn

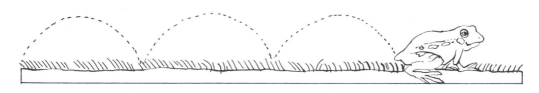

45

The Blind Men
and the Elephant

It was six men of Indostan
  To learning much inclined,
Who went to see the elephant
  (Though all of them were blind),
That each by observation
  Might satisfy his mind.

The *First* approached the elephant,
  And, happening to fall
Against his broad and sturdy side,
  At once began to bawl:
"God bless me! but the elephant
  Is very like a wall!"

The *Second*, feeling of the tusk,
  Cried, "Ho! what have we here
So very round and smooth and
    sharp?
  To me 'tis mighty clear
This wonder of an elephant
  Is very like a spear!"

The *Third* approached the animal,
  And happening to take
The squirming trunk within his
    hands,
  Thus boldly up and spake:
"I see," quoth he, "the elephant
  Is very like a snake!"

The *Fourth* reached out an eager
    hand,
  And felt about the knee.

"What most this wondrous beast is
    like
  Is mighty plain," quoth he;
" 'Tis clear enough the elephant
  Is very like a tree!"

The *Fifth*, who chanced to touch the
    ear,
  Said: "E'en the blindest man
Can tell what this resembles most;
  Deny the fact who can,
This marvel of an elephant
  Is very like a fan!"

The *Sixth* no sooner had begun
  About the beast to grope,
Then, seizing on the swinging tail
  That fell within his scope,
"I see," quoth he, "the elephant
  Is very like a rope!"

And so these men of Indostan
  Disputed loud and long,
Each in his own opinion
  Exceeding stiff and strong,
Though each was partly in the right,
  And all were in the wrong!

The Moral:
So, oft in theologic wars,
  The disputants, I ween,
Rail on in utter ignorance
  Of what each other mean,
And prate about an elephant
  Not one of them has seen!

John Godfrey Saxe

The Difference

'Twixt optimist and pessimist
The difference is droll:
The optimist sees the doughnut;
The pessimist sees the hole.

Tremendous Trifles

For want of a nail, the shoe was lost;
For want of the shoe, the horse was
    lost;
For want of the horse, the rider was
    lost;
For want of the rider, the battle was
    lost;
For want of the battle, the kingdom
    was lost;
And all from the want of a horseshoe
    nail.

Waste not, want not, is a maxim I
    would teach.
Let your watchword be dispatch,
    and practice what you preach;
Do not let your chances like
    sunbeams pass you by,
For you never miss the water till the
    well runs dry.

Rowland Howard

He that heareth my word,
and believeth on him that sent me,
    hath everlasting life,
and shall not come into
    condemnation;
but is passed from death unto life.

The Bible, John 5:24

Be sure your sin will find you out.

The Bible, Numbers 32:23

However they talk, whatever they
    say,
Look straight at the task without
    dismay —
And if you can do it, do it today.

*Adapted from the German by
Louis Untermeyer*

The words of a wise man's mouth are
gracious.

The Bible, Ecclesiastes 10:12

It is a good thing to give thanks
unto the Lord, and to sing praises
unto thy name, O most High.

The Bible, Psalm 92:1

One reason a dog is such a lovable
creature is that his tail wags instead
of his tongue.

Willful waste brings woeful want
And you may live to pay.
How I wish I had that crust
That once I threw away.

Mother Goose

To sleep easy at night,
Let your supper be light,
Or else you'll complain
Of a stomach in pain.

Mother Goose

Character

Let me be a little kinder,
Let me be a little blinder
  To the faults of those about me;
  Let me praise a little more.
Let me be, when I am weary,
Just a little bit more cheery;
  Let me serve a little better
  Those that I am striving for.

Let me be a little braver
When temptation bids me waver;
  Let me strive a little harder
  To be all that I should be.
Let me be a little meeker
With the brother that is weaker;
  Let me think more of my neighbor
  And a little less of me.

(My Daily Creed)

A Psalm of Life

Tell me not, in mournful numbers,
  "Life is but an empty dream!"
For the soul is dead that slumbers,
  And things are not what they
    seem.

Life is real! Life is earnest!
  And the grave is not its goal;
"Dust thou art, to dust returnest,"
  Was not spoken of the soul.

Not enjoyment, and not sorrow,
  Is our destined end or way;
But to act, that each to-morrow
  Find us farther than to-day.

Art is long, and Time is fleeting,
  And our hearts, though stout and
    brave,
Still, like muffled drums are beating
  Funeral marches to the grave.

In the world's broad field of battle,
  In the bivouac of Life,
Be not like dumb, driven cattle;
  Be a hero in the strife!

Trust no Future, howe'er pleasant!
  Let the dead Past bury its dead!
Act, — act in the living Present!
  Heart within, and God o'erhead!

Lives of great men all remind us
  We can make our lives sublime,
And, departing, leave behind us
  Footprints on the sands of time!

Footprints, that perhaps another,
  Sailing o'er life's solemn main,
A forlorn and shipwrecked brother,
  Seeing, shall take heart again.

Let us, then, be up and doing,
  With a heart for any fate;
Still achieving, still pursuing,
  Learn to labor and to wait.

Henry Wadsworth Longfellow

I Would Be True

I would be true, for there are those
  who trust me;
I would be pure, for there are those
  who care;
I would be strong, for there is much
  to suffer;
I would be brave, for there is much
  to dare.

I would be friend of all — the foe, the
  friendless;
I would be giving, and forget the
  gift;
I would be humble, for I know my
  weakness;
I would look up, and laugh, and
  love, and lift.

I would be learning, day by day, the
  lessons
My heavenly Father gives me in His
  Word;
I would be quick to hear His lightest
  whisper,
And prompt and glad to do the
  things I've heard.

Howard Arnold Walter

An Ancient Prayer

Give me a good digestion, Lord,
  and also something to digest.
Give me a healthy body, Lord,
  and sense to keep it at its best.
Give me a healthy mind, good Lord,
  to keep the good and pure in sight,
Which, seeing sin, is not appalled,
  but finds a way to set it right.

Give me a mind that is not bound,
  that does not whimper, whine,
    or sigh.
Don't let me worry overmuch about
  the fussy thing called I.
Give me a sense of humor, Lord;
  give me the grace to see a joke,
To get some happiness from life
  and pass it on to other folk.

Thomas H. B. Webb

Young men! let the nobleness of your mind impel you to its improvement. You are too strong to be defeated, save by yourselves.

Refuse to live merely to eat and sleep. Brutes can do these, but you are men. Act the part of men.

Prepare yourselves to endure toil. Resolve to rise; you have but to resolve. Nothing can hinder your success if you determine to succeed.

Do not waste your time by wishing and dreaming, but go earnestly to work.

Let nothing discourage you. If you have but little time, improve that little; if you have no books, borrow them; if you have no teachers, teach yourself; if your early education has been neglected, by the greater diligence repair the defect.

Let not a craven heart or a love of ease rob you of the inestimable benefit of self-culture.

Labor faithfully, labor fearlessly, and look to God, who giveth wisdom and upbraideth not, and you shall reap a harvest more valuable than gold or jewels.

W. D. Howard

A man of words and not of deeds
Is like a garden full of weeds;
And when the weeds begin to grow
It's like a garden full of snow;
And when the snow begins to fall
It's like a bird upon the wall;
And when the bird begins to fly
It's like an eagle in the sky;
And when the sky begins to roar
It's like a lion at the door;
And when the door begins to crack
It's like a stick across your back;
And when your back begins to smart
It's like a penknife in your heart;
And when your heart begins to
     bleed
You're dead, and dead, and dead in-
     deed.

Be Strong

Be strong!
We are not here to play, to dream, to
     drift;
We have hard work to do and loads
     to lift;
Shun not the struggle — face it; 'tis
     God's gift.

Be strong!
Say not, "The days are evil. Who's to
     blame?"
And fold the hands and acquiesce —
     oh, shame!
Stand up, speak out, and bravely, in
     God's name.

Be strong!
It matters not how deep entrenched
     the wrong,
How hard the battle goes, the day
     how long;
Faint not — fight on! Tomorrow
     comes the song.

Maltbie D. Babcock

A Child's Creed

I believe in God above;
I believe in Jesus' love;
I believe His Spirit, too,
Comes to teach me what to do;
I believe that I must be
True and good, dear Lord, like Thee.

Courage

Dare to be true;
   Nothing can need a lie;
The fault that needs one most
   Grows two thereby.

George Herbert

Today

The best thing you have in this world is Today. Today is your savior; it is often crucified between two thieves, Yesterday and Tomorrow.

Today you can be happy, not Yesterday or borrowed from Tomorrow. There is no happiness except Today's.

Most of our misery is left over from Yesterday or borrowed from Tomorrow. Keep Today clean. Make up your mind to enjoy your food, your work, your play Today anyhow. . . .

Today is yours. God has given it to you. All your Yesterdays He has taken back. All your Tomorrows are still in His hands.

Today is yours. Take its pleasures and be glad. Take its pains and play the man. . . .

Today is yours. Use it so that at its close you can say:

I have lived, and loved, Today!

Frank Crane

How Did You Die?

Did you tackle that trouble that came
    your way
    With a resolute heart and
      cheerful?
Or hide your face from the light of
    day
    With a craven soul and fearful?
Oh, a trouble's a ton, or a trouble's
    an ounce,
    Or a trouble is what you make it,
And it isn't the fact that you're hurt
    that counts,
    But only how did you take it?

You are beaten to earth? Well, well,
    what's that?
    Come up with a smiling face.

It's nothing against you to fall down
    flat,
    But to lie there — that's disgrace.
The harder you're thrown, why the
    higher you bounce;
    Be proud of your blackened eye!
It isn't the fact that you're licked that
    counts;
    It's how did you fight — and why?

And though you be done to the
    death, what then?
    If you battled the best you could;
If you played your part in the world
    of men,
    Why, the Critic will call it good.
Death comes with a crawl, or comes
    with a pounce,
    And whether he's slow or spry,
It isn't the fact that you're dead that
    counts,
    But only, how did you die?

Edmund Vance Cooke

Question not, but live and labour
    Till your goal be won,
Helping every feeble neighbour,
    Seeking help from none;
Life is mostly froth and bubble,
    Two things stand like stone —
Kindness in another's trouble,
    Courage in our own.

Adam Lindsay Gordon

I am not bound to win,
But I am bound to be true.
I am not bound to succeed,
But I am bound to live up to what
    light I have.
I must stand with anybody that
    stands right
And part with him when he goes
    wrong.

Abraham Lincoln

Eldorado

Gaily bedight,
 A gallant knight,
In sunshine and in shadow,
 Had journeyed long,
 Singing a song,
In search of Eldorado.

But he grew old —
 This knight so bold —
And o'er his heart a shadow
 Fell as he found
 No spot of ground
That looked like Eldorado.

And, as his strength
 Failed him at length,
He met a pilgrim shadow —
 "Shadow," said he,
 "Where can it be —
This land of Eldorado?"

"Over the Mountains
 Of the Moon,
Down the Valley of the Shadow,
 Ride, boldly ride,"
 The shade replied —
"If you seek for Eldorado!"

Edgar Allen Poe

Oh, Adam was a gardener, and God
 who made him sees
That half a proper gardener's work
 is done upon his knees.
So when your work is finished,
 you can wash your hands
 and pray
For the glory of that garden,
 that it may not pass away.

Rudyard Kipling
(from The Glory of the Garden)

My heart leaps up when I behold
 A rainbow in the sky:
So was it when my life began;
So is it now I am a man;
So be it when I shall grow old,
 Or let me die!

William Wordsworth

Dear God,
When someone tries to make me do
What I am sure would not please
 You,
Do help me then to be so strong
That I just couldn't do the wrong.

Garry Cleveland Myers

Make a joyful noise unto the Lord,
 all ye lands.
Serve the Lord with gladness:
Come before his presence
 with singing.
Know ye that the Lord he is God:
It is he that hath made us,
 and not we ourselves;
We are his people, and the sheep
 of his pasture.
Enter into his gates with thanks-
 giving,
And into his courts with praise:
Be thankful unto him, and bless his
 name.
For the Lord is good;
 his mercy is everlasting;
And his truth endureth to all
 generations.

The Bible, Psalm 100

Courtesy and Graces

I'll be polite in many ways
And kindness show to others,
My parents, friends, and neighbors
        too,
My sister and my brother.

I'll run on errands when I can,
Sweep the walk, rake the leaves;
I'll carry groceries from the car,
Say "Thanks" and "If you please."

When company comes I'll gladly
        share
My books and all my toys;
And if there's grownup visitors
I'll not make too much noise.

At mealtime I will bow my head
And wait till prayer is said;
Sometimes I'll say the prayer myself:
"Thanks, dear God, for our bread."

(I'll Be Polite)
Lloyd E. Werth

Courtesy

Courtesy is a quality of soul refinement impossible to purchase, impossible to acquire at easy cost.

Politeness is but the shallow imitation of courtesy, and often masquerades as a refining quality in life when it is courtesy that truly refines mankind. Politeness can be assumed, courtesy never. One can be trained upon the surface of the mind, the other must be born in the soul.

Noble natures are often impolite, often lack surface politeness, but have real courtesy in the soul, where great and good men really live. They would not stoop to low cunning or contemptible meanness.

Polite people may be the very quintessence of cunning, so artful that the world regards them as delightful people until their shallow souls are uncovered. The difference between the polite person and the courteous soul is as wide as the gulf that separates evil from good.

F. E. Elwell

Hurt No Living Thing

Hurt no living thing:
　Ladybird, nor butterfly,
Nor moth with dusty wing,
　Nor cricket chirping cheerily,
Nor grasshopper so light of leap,
　Nor dancing gnat, nor beetle fat,
Nor harmless worms that creep.

Christina Rossetti

Don't look for the flaws as you go
　through life,
And even if you find them,
Be wise and kind and somewhat
　blind
And look for the good behind them.

Kindness is a language which the blind can see and the deaf can hear.

Important Words

The Four Most Important Words:
　"It was my fault."
The Three Most Important Words:
　"If you please."
The Two Most Important Words:
　"Thank you."
The One Most Important Word:
　"We."
The Least Important Word:
　"I."

Politeness is to do and say
The kindest thing in the kindest
　way.

Kindness to Animals

Little children, never give
Pain to things that feel and live;
Let the gentle robin come
For the crumbs you save at home, —
As his meat you throw along
He'll repay you with a song;
Never hurt the timid hare
Peeping from her green grass lair,
Let her come and sport and play
On the lawn at close of day;
The little lark goes soaring high
To the bright windows of the sky,
Singing as if 'twere always spring,
And fluttering on an untired
　wing, —
Oh! let him sing his happy song,
Nor do these gentle creatures wrong.

56

Table Manners I

The Goops they lick their fingers,
  And the Goops they lick their
    knives;
They spill their broth on the
    tablecloth —
  Oh, they lead disgusting lives!
The Goops they talk while eating,
  And loud and fast they chew;
And that is why I'm glad that I
  Am not a Goop — are you?

Table Manners II

The Goops are gluttonous and rude,
  They gug and gumble with their
    food;
They throw their crumbs upon the
    floor,
  And at dessert they tease for more;
They will not eat their soup and
    bread
  But like to gobble sweets, instead;
And this is why I oft decline,
  When I am asked to stay and dine!

Gelett Burgess

Courtesy Hints

Use good table manners.
Don't interrupt your parents when
    they are talking.
Say "please" and "thank you."
Say "excuse me" when you bump
    into someone.

Beautiful faces are they that wear
The light of a pleasant spirit there;
Beautiful hands are they that do
Deeds that are noble, good, and
    true;
Beautiful feet are they that go
Swiftly to lighten another's woe.

Keep this in mind, and all will go
    right
As on your way you go;
Be sure you know about all you tell
But don't tell all you know.

If you must yawn, just turn aside
And with your hand the motion
    hide.
And when you blow your nose, be
    brief;
And neatly use your handkerchief.

Of Courtesy

Good Manners may in Seven Words
    be found:
Forget Yourself and Think of Those
    Around.
                    Arthur Guiterman

Manners are the happy way of doing
    things.
Your manners are always under
    examination.

                    Ralph Waldo Emerson

Courtesy Tips

Be helpful
Be nice
Talk proper
Smile

Talking to God

I close my eyes and bow my head
When a grace or prayer is said.
I wouldn't stir or even nod
When other persons talk to God.

Garry Cleveland Myers

Hearts, Like Doors

Hearts, like doors,
    will open with ease
To very very little
    keys,
And don't forget that
    two of these
Are "Thank you, Sir,"
    and "If you please."

Robert Louis Stevenson

Golden Keys

A bunch of golden keys is mine
To make each day with gladness
    shine.
"Good Morning!" that's the golden
    key
That unlocks every day for me.
When evening comes, "Good
    Night!" I say
And close the door of each glad day.
When at the table "If you please,"
I take from off my bunch of keys.
When friends give anything to me,
I'll use my little "Thank you" key.
"Excuse me," "Beg your pardon,"
    too,
If by mistake some harm I do.
Or if unkindly harm I've given
With "Forgive me" key I'll be
    forgiven.
On a golden ring these keys I'll bind;
This is its motto: "Be ye kind."
I'll often use each golden key,
And so a happy child, polite I'll be.

Whole Duty of Children

A child should always say what's
    true,
And speak when he is spoken to,
And behave mannerly at table —
At least as far as he is able.

Robert Louis Stevenson

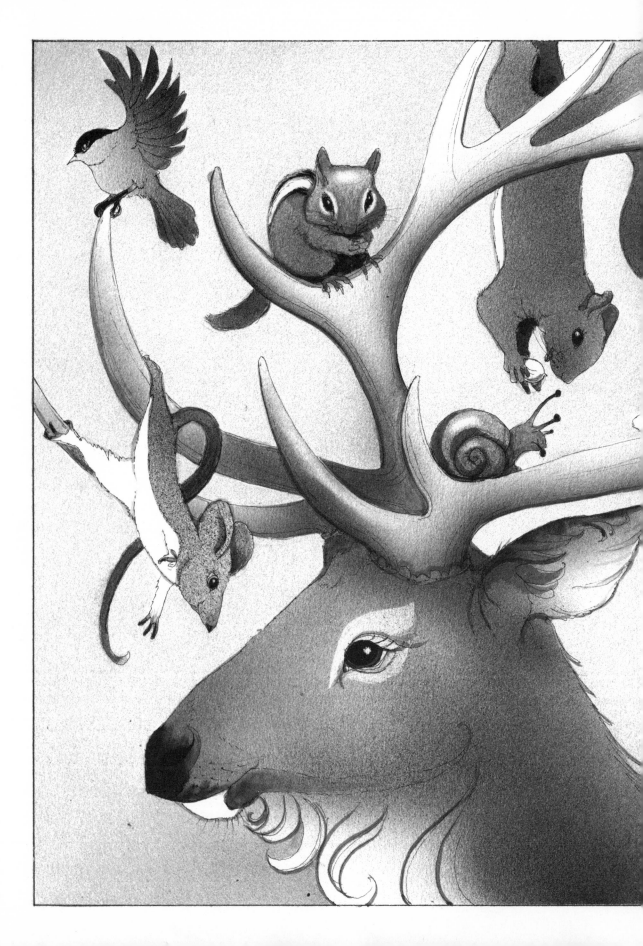

Creatures of Every Kind

I think mice
Are rather nice.

Their tails are long,
Their faces small,
They haven't any
Chins at all.
Their ears are pink,
Their teeth are white,
They run about
The house at night.
They nibble things
They shouldn't touch
And no one seems
To like them much.

But *I* think mice
Are nice.

(Mice)
Rose Fyleman

Mary's Lamb

Mary had a little lamb,
  Its fleece was white as snow,
And every where that Mary went
  The lamb was sure to go;
He followed her to school one day —
  That was against the rule,
It made the children laugh and play,
  To see a lamb at school.

And so the Teacher turned him out,
  But still he lingered near,
And waited patiently about,
  Till Mary did appear;
And then he ran to her, and laid
  His head upon her arm,
As if he said — "I'm not afraid —
  You'll keep me from all harm."

"What makes the lamb love Mary
    so?"
  The eager children cry —
"O, Mary loves the lamb, you
    know,"
  The Teacher did reply —
"And you each gentle animal
  In confidence may bind,
And make them follow at your call,
  If you are always kind."

Sarah Josepha Hale

The Cow

The friendly cow all red and white,
  I love with all my heart;
She gives me cream, with all her
    might,
  To eat with apple-tart.

She wanders lowing here and there,
  And yet she cannot stray,
All in the pleasant open air,
  The pleasant light of day.

And blown by all the winds that pass
  And wet with all the showers,
She walks among the meadow grass
  And eats the meadow flowers.

Robert Louis Stevenson

Chanticleer

High and proud on the barnyard
    fence
Walks rooster in the morning.
He shakes his comb, he shakes his
    tail
And gives his daily warning.

"Get up, you lazy boys and girls,
It's time you should be dressing!"
I wonder if he keeps a clock,
Or if he's only guessing.

John Farrar

My Hairy Dog

My dog's so furry I've not seen
His face for years and years:
His eyes are buried out of sight,
I only guess his ears.

When people ask me for his breed,
I do not know or care:
He has the beauty of them all
Hidden beneath his hair.

Herbert Asquith

The Hippopotamus

In the squdgy river,
  Down the oozely bank,
Where the ripples shiver,
  And the reeds are rank.

Where the purple Kippo
  Makes an awful fuss,
Lives the Hip-hip-hippo
  Hippo-pot-a-mus!

Broad his back and steady;
  Broad and flat his nose;
Sharp and keen and ready
  Little eyes are those.

You would think him dreaming
  Where the mud is deep.
It is only seeming —
  He is not asleep.

Better not disturb him,
  There'd be an awful fuss
If you touched the Hippo,
  Hippo-pot-a-mus.

Georgia Roberts Durston

The Snail's Dream

A snail who had a way, it seems,
Of dreaming very curious dreams,
Once dreamt he was — you'll never
    guess! —
The Lightning Limited Express.

Oliver Herford

Eletelephony

Once there was an elephant,
Who tried to use the telephant —
No! No! I mean an elephone
Who tried to use the telephone —
(Dear me! I am not certain quite
That even now I've got it right.)

Howe'er it was, he got his trunk
Entangled in the telephunk;
The more he tried to get it free,
The louder buzzed the telephee —
(I fear I'd better drop the song
Of elephop and telephong!)

Laura E. Richards

Trot Along, Pony

Trot along, pony.
  Late in the day,
Down by the meadow
  Is the loveliest way.

The apples are rosy
  And ready to fall.
The branches hang over
  By Grandfather's wall.

But the red sun is sinking
  Away out of sight.
The chickens are settling
  Themselves for the night.

Your stable is waiting
  And supper will come.
So turn again, pony,
  Turn again home.

Marion Edey and Dorothy Grider

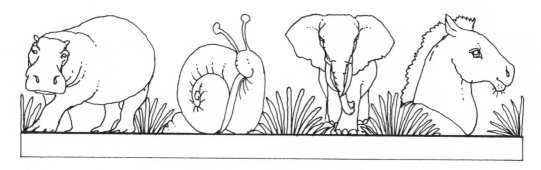

63

Lion Thoughts

I wouldn't like at all to be
A lion in a zoo,
With people standing there to see
The lion things I do.

I'd rather be in jungle land,
Beneath a jungle tree,
With only jungle animals
To stand and look at me.

Iowna Elizabeth Banker

The Seals

The seals all flap
Their shining flips
And bounce balls on
Their nosey tips,
And beat a drum,
And catch a bar,
And wriggle with
How pleased they are.

Dorothy Aldis

Once I Saw a Little Bird

Once I saw a little bird
    Come hop, hop, hop;
So I cried, "Little bird,
    Will you stop, stop, stop?"

And was going to the window
    To say, "How do you do?"
But he shook his little tail,
    And far away he flew.

The Squirrel

Whisky, frisky,
Hippity hop,
Up he goes
To the tree top!

Whirly, twirly,
Round and round,
Down he scampers
To the ground.

Furly, curly,
What a tail!
Tall as a feather,
Broad as a sail!

Where's his supper?
In the shell,
Snappity, crackity,
Out it fell!

Catkin

I have a little pussy,
    And her coat is silver gray;
She lives in a great wide meadow
    And she never runs away.
She always is a pussy,
    She'll never be a cat
Because — she's a pussy willow!
    Now what do you think of that!

Pussy has a whiskered face,
Kitty has such pretty ways;
Doggie scampers when I call,
And has a heart to love us all.

Christina Rossetti

64

The Happy Sheep

All through the night the happy
        sheep
Lie in the meadow grass asleep.

Their wool keeps out the frost and
        rain
Until the sun comes round again.

They have no buttons to undo,
Nor hair to brush, like me and you.

And with the light they lift their
        heads
To find their breakfast on their beds,

Or rise and walk about and eat
The carpet underneath their feet.

Wilfred Thorley

Did you ever have a chipmunk for a
        friend?
    I have one that I call "Chippy."
Sometimes he comes right on my
        lap,
    If I put bread there,
    And stay very still.
    Then he sits up,
And holds the bread in his thin
        brown fingers,
Turning it over and over as he eats,
And watching me with his round,
        bright eye,
And listening with his tiny ears.
    If I even so much as breathe,
He stuffs the bread in his cheek and
        scampers off.

Jessie Orton Jones
(XII from Secrets)

The Eagle

He clasps the crag with crooked
        hands;
Close to the sun in lonely lands,
Ringed with the azure world, he
        stands.

The wrinkled sea beneath him
        crawls;
He watches from his mountain
        walls,
And like a thunderbolt he falls.

Alfred Tennyson

What Is It?

Tall ears,
Twinkly nose,
Tiny tail,
And — hop, he goes!

What *is* he —
Can you guess?
I feed him carrots
And watercress.

His ears are long,
His tail is small —
And he doesn't make any
Noise at all!

Tall ears,
Twinkly nose,
Tiny tail,
And — hop, he goes!

Marie Louise Allen

The Caterpillar

Brown and furry
Caterpillar, in a hurry
Take your walk
To the shady leaf or stalk
Or what not,
Which may be the chosen spot.
No toad spy you,
Hovering bird of prey pass by you;
Spin and die,
To live again a butterfly.

Christina Rossetti

I Love Little Pussy

I love little Pussy,
    Her coat is so warm,
And if I don't hurt her,
    She'll do me no harm;
So I'll not pull her tail,
    Nor drive her away,
But Pussy and I
    Very gently will play.

Jane Taylor

The Hummingbird

The hummingbird, the
    hummingbird,
    So fairy-like and bright;
It lives among the sunny flowers,
    A creature of delight.

Mary Howitt

Choosing a Kitten

A black-nosed kitten will slumber all
    the day;
A white-nosed kitten is ever glad to
    play;
A yellow-nosed kitten will answer to
    your call;
And a gray-nosed kitten I like best of
    all.

Little Robin Red-Breast

Little Robin Red-breast sat upon a
    tree,
Up went Pussy-cat, and down went
    he;
Down came Pussy-cat, and away
    Robin ran;
Says little Robin Red-breast,
"Catch me if you can."

Little Robin Red-breast jumped
    upon a wall,
Pussy-cat jumped after him, and
    almost got a fall;
Little Robin chirped and sang,
And what did Pussy say?
Pussy-cat said "Mew," and Robin
    flew away.

Angleworms

I like to watch an angleworm.
He moves with such a funny squirm.
He stretches thin and long, and then
Gets quite short and fat again.

A robin likes him for a meal —
Though he's wiggle-y to feel!
On my hand, he twists and squirms,
But I do like angleworms!

Marie Louise Allen

The Humble Bee

Wiser far than human seer,
    Yellow-breeched philosopher!
Seeing only what is fair,
    Sipping only what is sweet,
Thou dost mock at fate and care.
    Leave the chaff, and take the
        wheat.

Ralph Waldo Emerson

Fuzzy wuzzy, creepy crawly
    Caterpillar funny,
You will be a butterfly
    When the days are sunny.

Lillian Schulz Vanada

The Grasshopper and the Elephant

Way down south where bananas
    grow,
A grasshopper stepped on an
    elephant's toe.
The elephant said, with tears in his
    eyes,
"Pick on somebody your own size."

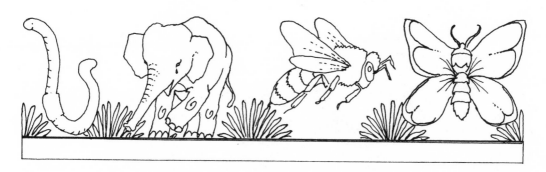

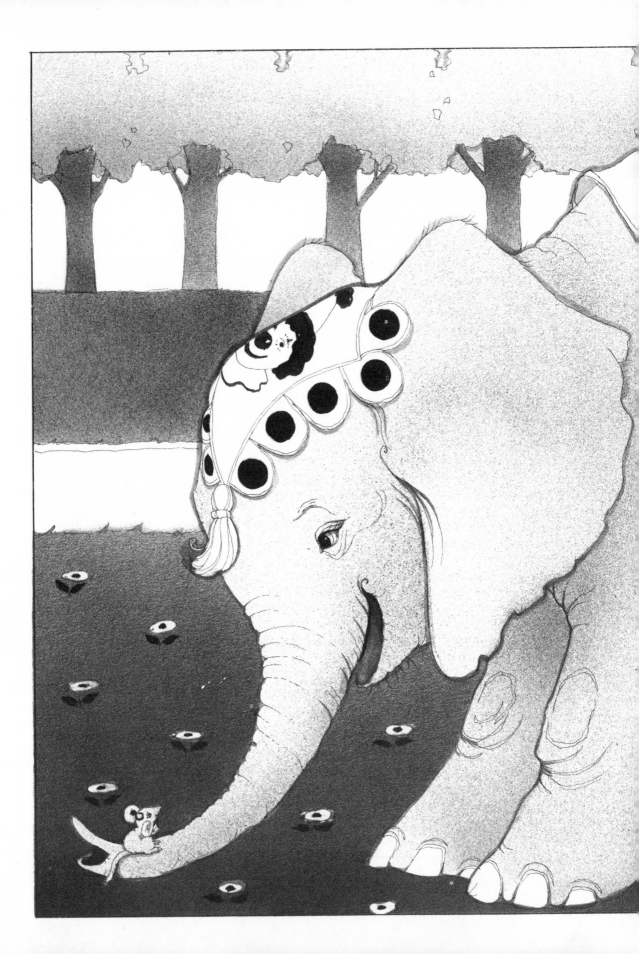

Curiosity

Does the Elephant remember,
In the gray light before dawn,
Old noises of the jungle
In mornings long gone?

Does the Elephant remember
The cry of hungry beasts;
The Tiger and the Leopard,
The Lion at his feasts?

Do his mighty eardrums listen
For the thunder of the feet
Of the Buffalo and Zebra
In the dark and dreadful heat?

Does His Majesty remember,
Does he stir himself and dream
Of the long-forgotten music
Of a long-forgotten stream?

(Circus Elephant)
Kathryn Worth

Why English Is So Hard!

We'll begin with a box, and the
  plural is boxes;
  But the plural of ox should be
    oxen, not oxes.
Then one fowl is goose, but two are
  called geese.
  Yet the plural of moose should
    never be meese.

You may find a lone mouse or a
  whole lot of mice,
  But the plural of house is houses,
    not hice.
If the plural of man is always called
  men,
  Why shouldn't the plural of pan be
    called pen?

The cow in the plural may be cows or
  kine,
  But the plural of vow is vows, not
    vine.
And I speak of a foot, and you show
  me your feet,
  But I give you a boot; would a pair
    be called beet?

If one is a tooth and a whole set are
  teeth,
  Why shouldn't the plural of booth
    be called beeth?
If the singular is this, and the plural
  is these,
  Should the plural of kiss be
    nicknamed kese?

That one may be that, and three may
  be those,
  Yet the plural of hat would never
    be hose;
We speak of a brother, and also of
  brethren,
  But though we say mother, we
    never say methren.

The masculine pronouns are he, his
  and him,
  But imagine the feminine she,
    shis and shim!
So our English, I think you will all
  agree,
  Is the trickiest language you ever
    did see.

The Fishing Pole

A fishing pole's a curious thing;
It's made of just a stick and string;
  A boy at one end and a wish;
  And on the other end a fish.

Mary Carolyn Davies

The Octopus

Tell me, O Octopus, I begs,
Is those things arms, or is they legs?
I marvel at thee, Octopus;
If I were thou, I'd call me Us.

Ogden Nash

If All the Seas Were One Sea

If all the seas were one sea,
What a *great* sea that would be!
And if all the trees were one tree,
What a *great* tree that would be!
And if all the axes were one axe,
What a *great* axe that would be!
And if all the men were one man,
What a *great* man he would be!
And if the *great* man took the *great*
  axe,
And cut down the *great* tree,
And let it fall into the *great* sea,
What a splish splash *that* would be!

70

A Pin Has a Head

A pin has a head, but has no hair;
A clock has a face, but no mouth
    there;
Needles have eyes, but they cannot
    see;
A fly has a trunk without lock or key;
A timepiece may lose, but cannot
    win;
A corn-field dimples without a chin;
A hill has no leg, but has a foot;
A wine-glass a stem, but not a root;
A watch has hands, but no thumb or
    finger;
A boot has a tongue, but is no
    singer;
Rivers run, though they have no
    feet;
A saw has teeth, but it does not eat;
Ash-trees have keys, yet never a
    lock;
And baby crows, without being a
    cock.

Christina Rossetti

Where Go the Boats?

Dark brown is the river,
    Golden is the sand.
It flows along forever,
    With trees on either hand.

Green leaves a-floating,
    Castles of the foam,
Boats of mine a-boating —
    Where will all come home?

On goes the river
    And out past the mill,
Away down the valley,
    Away down the hill.

Away down the river,
    A hundred miles or more,
Other little children
    Shall bring my boats ashore.

Robert Louis Stevenson

How Doth the Little Crocodile

How doth the little crocodile
    Improve his shining tail,
And pour the waters of the Nile
    On every golden scale!

How cheerfully he seems to grin,
    How neatly spreads his claws,
And welcomes little fishes in
    With gently smiling jaws!

Lewis Carroll

Sandpile Town

It took at least a morning
of working in the sun
and even then our village
was just a sandpile one —
the roads beyond the suburbs
were only just begun,
the little lakes we put in
were only just-for-fun —
how long it must have taken,
how long it must have taken,
how long it must have **taken**
before the World got done!

Aileen Fisher

71

Who Taught Them?

Who taught the bird to build her
  nest
  Of softest wool and hay and moss,
Who taught her how to weave it
  best,
  And lay the tiny twigs across?

Who taught the busy bee to fly
  Among the sweetest herbs and
    flowers;
And lay her store of honey by,
  Providing food for winter hours?

Who taught the little ant the way
  Her narrow hole so well to bore?
And through the pleasant summer
    day,
  To gather up her winter's store?

'Twas God that taught them all the
  way,
  And gave these little creatures
    skill;
And teaches children if they pray,
  To know and do His holy will.

I Often Pause and Wonder

I often pause and wonder
At fate's peculiar ways;
For nearly all our famous men
    were born on holidays.

Moles

Don't you feel sorry
for grubby old moles,
always in tunnels,
always in holes,
never out watching
the sun climb high
or the grass bend low
or the wind race by
or stars make twinkles
all over the sky?

Aileen Fisher

How They Sleep

Some things go to sleep in such a
  funny way:
Little birds stand on one leg and tuck
  their heads away;

Chickens do the same, standing on
  their perch;
Little mice lie soft and still, as if they
  were in church;

Kittens curl up close in such a funny
  ball;
Horses hang their sleepy heads and
  stand still in a stall;

Sometimes dogs stretch out, or curl
  up in a heap;
Cows lie down upon their sides
  when they would go to sleep.

But little babies dear are snugly
  tucked in beds,
Warm with blankets, all so soft, and
  pillows for their heads.

Bird and beast and babe — I wonder
  which of all
Dream the dearest dreams that down
  from dreamland fall!

What Robin Told

How do robins build their nests?
  Robin Redbreast told me —
First a wisp of yellow hay
In a pretty round they lay;

Then some shreds of downy floss,
Feathers, too, and bits of moss,
Woven with a sweet, sweet song,
This way, that way, and across;
  THAT'S what Robin told me.

Where do robins hide their nests?
  Robin Redbreast told me —
Up among the leaves so deep,
Where the sunbeams rarely creep,
Long before the leaves are gold,
Bright-eyed stars will peep and see
Baby robins — one, two, three;
  THAT'S what Robin told me.

George Cooper

72

The Naughty Boy

There was a naughty boy,
  And a naughty boy was he,
He ran away to Scotland
  The people for to see —
    Then he found
    That the ground
    Was as hard,
    That a yard
    Was as long,
    That a song
    Was as merry,
    That a cherry
    Was as red,
    That lead
    Was as weighty,
    That fourscore
    Was as eighty,
    That a door
    Was as wooden
    As in England —
So he stood in his shoes
  And he wondered,
  He wondered.
He stood in his shoes
  And he wondered.

John Keats

A Centipede

A centipede was happy quite
Until a frog in fun
Said, "Pray, which leg comes after
  which?"
This raised her mind to such a pitch,
She lay distracted in a ditch,
Considering how to run.

Flower in the Crannied Wall

Flower in the crannied wall,
I pluck you out of the crannies,
I hold you here, root and all, in my
  hand,
Little flower — but if I could
  understand
What you are, root and all, and all in
  all,
I should know what God and man is.

Alfred Tennyson

Whistles

I want to learn to whistle.
I've always wanted to.
I fix my mouth to do it but
The whistle won't come through.

I think perhaps it's stuck, and so
I try it once again.
Can people swallow whistles?
Where is my whistle then?

Dorothy Aldis

How Doth the Little Busy Bee

How doth the little busy bee
  Improve each shining hour,
And gather honey all the day
  From every passing flower!

How skillfully she builds her cell;
  How neat she spreads the wax!
And labors hard to store it well
  With the sweet food she makes.

Isaac Watts

Favorites

By the shores of Gitche Gumee,
By the shining Big-Sea-Water,
Stood the wigwam of Nokomis,
Daughter of the Moon, Nokomis.
Dark behind it rose the forest,
Rose the black and gloomy pine-
      trees,
Rose the firs with cones upon them;
Bright before it beat the water,
Beat the clear and sunny water,
Beat the shining Big-Sea-Water.
   There the wrinkled, old Nokomis
Nursed the little Hiawatha,
Rocked him in his linden cradle,
Bedded soft in moss and rushes,
Safely bound with reindeer sinews;
Stilled his fretful wail by saying,
"Hush! the Naked Bear will hear
      thee!"
Lulled him into slumber, singing,
"Ewa-yea! my little owlet!
Who is this, that lights the wigwam?
With his great eyes lights the
      wigwam?
Ewa-yea! my little owlet!"

Many things Nokomis taught him
Of the stars that shine in heaven;
Showed him Ishkoodah, the comet,
   Ishkoodah, with fiery tresses;
Showed the Death-Dance of the
   spirits,
Warriors with their plumes and
   war-clubs,
Flaring far away to northward
In the frosty nights of Winter;
Showed the broad, white road in
   heaven,
Pathway of the ghosts, the shadows,
Running   straight   across   the
   heavens,
Crowded with the ghosts, the
   shadows.
   At the door on summer evenings
Sat the little Hiawatha;
Heard the whispering of the pine-
   trees,
Heard the lapping of the water,
Sounds of music, words of wonder;
"Minne-wawa!" said the pine-trees,
"Mudway-aushka!" said the water.
   Saw the fire-fly, Wah-wah-taysee,
Flitting through the dusk of
   evening,
With the twinkle of its candle
Lighting up the brakes and bushes,
And he sang the song of children,
Sang the song Nokomis taught him:
"Wah-wah-taysee, little fire-fly,
Little, flitting, white-fire insect,
Little, dancing, white-fire creature,
Light me with your little candle,
Ere upon my bed I lay me,
Ere in sleep I close my eyelids!"
   Saw the moon rise from the water,
Rippling, rounding from the water,
Saw the flecks and shadows on it,
Whispered, "What is that,
   Nokomis?"
And the good Nokomis answered:
"Once a warrior, very angry,
Seized his grandmother, and threw
   her
Up into the sky at midnight;
Right against the moon he threw
   her;
'Tis her body that you see there."

Saw the rainbow in the heavens,
In the eastern sky, the rainbow,
Whispered, "What is that,
   Nokomis?"
And the good Nokomis answered:
" 'Tis the heaven of flowers you see
   there;
All the wild-flowers of the forest,
All the lilies of the prairie,
When on earth they fade and perish,
Blossom in that heaven above us."
   When he heard the owls at
      midnight,
Hooting, laughing in the forest,
"What is that?" he cried in terror;
"What is that?" he said,
   "Nokomis?"
And the good Nokomis answered:
"That is but the owl and owlet,
Talking in their native language,
Talking, scolding at each other."
   Then the little Hiawatha
Learned of every bird its language,
Learned their names and all their
   secrets,
How they built their nests in
   Summer,
Where they hid themselves in
   Winter,
Talked with them whene'er he met
   them,
Called them "Hiawatha's
   Chickens."
   Of all beasts he learned the
      language,
Learned their names and all their
   secrets,
How the beavers built their lodges,
Where the squirrels hid their acorns,
How the reindeer ran so swiftly,
Why the rabbit was so timid,
Talked with them whene'er he met
   them,
Called them "Hiawatha's Brothers."

(Hiawatha's Childhood)
Henry Wadsworth Longfellow

76

The Village Blacksmith

Under a spreading chestnut tree
  The village smithy stands;
The smith, a mighty man is he,
  With large and sinewy hands;
And the muscles of his brawny arms
  Are strong as iron bands.

His hair is crisp, and black, and
    long,
  His face is like the tan;
His brow is wet with honest sweat,
  He earns whate'er he can,
And looks the whole world in the
    face,
  For he owes not any man.

Week in, week out, from morn till
    night,
  You can hear his bellows blow;
You can hear him swing his heavy
    sledge,
  With measured beat and slow,
Like a sexton ringing the village bell,
  When the evening sun is low.

And children coming home from
    school
  Look in at the open door;
They love to see the flaming forge,
  And hear the bellows roar,
And catch the burning sparks that
    fly
  Like chaff from a threshing floor.

He goes on Sunday to the church,
  And sits among his boys;
He hears the parson pray and
    preach,
  He hears his daughter's voice,
Singing in the village choir,
  And it makes his heart rejoice.

It sounds to him like her mother's
    voice,
  Singing in Paradise!
He needs must think of her once
    more,
  How in the grave she lies;
And with his hard, rough hand he
    wipes
  A tear out of his eyes.

Toiling — rejoicing — sorrowing,
  Onward through life he goes;
Each morning sees some task begin,
  Each evening sees it close;
Something attempted, something
    done,
  Has earned a night's repose.

Thanks, thanks to thee, my worthy
    friend,
  For the lesson thou has taught!
Thus at the flaming forge of life
  Our fortunes must be wrought;
Thus on its sounding anvil shaped
  Each burning deed and thought!

Henry Wadsworth Longfellow

The Bugle Song

The splendor falls on castle walls
And snowy summits old in story:
The long light shakes across the
    lakes,
And the wild cataract leaps in glory.

Blow, bugle, blow,
Set the wild echoes flying,
Blow, bugle; answer, echoes,
Dying, dying, dying.

O hark, O hear! how thin and clear,
And thinner, clearer, farther going!
O sweet and far from cliff and scar
The horns of Elfland faintly blowing!

Blow, let us hear,
The purple glens replying:
Blow, bugle; answer, echoes,
Dying, dying, dying.

O love, they die in yon rich sky,
They faint on hill or field or river:
Our echoes roll from soul to soul,
And grow for ever and for ever.

Blow, bugle, blow,
Set the wild echoes flying,
And answer, echoes, answer,
Dying, dying, dying.

Alfred Tennyson
(from The Princess)

The Apostles' Creed

I believe in God the Father
    Almighty,
  Maker of heaven and earth.
And in Jesus Christ, His Son, our
    Lord;
Who was conceived by the Holy
    Ghost,
Born of the Virgin Mary,
Suffered under Pontius Pilate,
Was crucified, dead, and buried;
He descended into hell;
The third day He arose from the
    dead;
He ascended into heaven,
And sitteth on the right hand of God
    the Father Almighty;
From thence He shall come to judge
    the quick and the dead.
I believe in the Holy Ghost;
The holy Christian Church; the
    communion of saints;
The forgiveness of sins;
The resurrection of the body;
And the life everlasting.
Amen.

Time to Rise

A birdie with a yellow bill
Hopped upon the window sill,
Cocked his shining eye and said:
"Ain't you 'shamed, you sleepy-
    head!"

Robert Louis Stevenson

I Can

So nigh is grandeur to our dust,
So near is God to man,
When Duty whispers low, *Thou
    must,*
The youth replies, *I can.*

Ralph Waldo Emerson
(from Voluntaries, III)

Old Ships

There is a memory stays upon old
    ships,
  A weightless cargo in the musty
    hold —
Of bright lagoons and prow-
    caressing lips,
  Of stormy midnights — and a tale
    untold.
They have remembered islands in
    the dawn,
  And windy capes that tried their
    slender spars,
And tortuous channels where their
    keels have gone,
  And calm blue nights of stillness
    and the stars.

Ah, never think that ships forget a
    shore,
  Or bitter seas, or winds that made
    them wise;
There is a dream upon them,
    evermore —
  And there be some who say that
    sunk ships rise
To seek familiar harbors in the
    night,
  Blowing in mists, their spectral
    sails like light.

David Morton

The Lord is my shepherd; I shall not
want.
He maketh me to lie down in green
pastures:
He leadeth me beside the still
waters.
He restoreth my soul:
He leadeth me in the paths of
righteousness for his name's
sake.
Yea, though I walk through the
valley of the shadow of death,
I will fear no evil: for thou art with
me;
Thy rod and thy staff they comfort
me.
Thou preparest a table before me in
the presence of mine enemies:
Thou anointest my head with oil; my
cup runneth over.
Surely goodness and mercy shall
follow me all the days of my
life:
And I will dwell in the house of the
Lord for ever.

The Bible, Psalm 23

The Destruction of Sennacherib

The Assyrian came down like the
wolf on the fold,
And his cohorts were gleaming in
purple and gold;
And the sheen of their spears was
like stars on the sea,
When the blue wave rolls nightly on
deep Galilee.

Like the leaves of the forest when
Summer is green,
That host with their banners at
sunset were seen;
Like the leaves of the forest when
Autumn hath blown,
That host on the morrow lay
wither'd and strown.

For the Angel of Death spread his
wings on the blast,
And breathed in the face of the foe as
he passed;
And the eyes of the sleepers waxed
deadly and chill,
And their hearts but once heaved,
and for ever grew still!

And there lay the steed with his
nostril all wide,
But through it there rolled not the
breath of his pride;
And the foam of his gasping lay
white on the turf,
And cold as the spray of the rock-
beating surf.

And there lay the rider distorted and
pale,
With the dew on his brow, and the
rust on his mail;
And the tents were all silent, the
banners alone,
The lances uplifted, the trumpet
unblown.

And the widows of Ashur are loud in
their wail,
And the idols are broken in the
temple of Baal;
And the might of the Gentile,
unsmote by the sword,
Hath melted like snow in the glance
of the Lord!

Lord Byron

Monday's child is fair of face,
Tuesday's child is full of grace,
Wednesday's child is full of woe,
Thursday's child has far to go,
Friday's child is loving and giving,
Saturday's child works hard for a
living,
But the child that is born on the
Sabbath day
Is blithe and bonny and good and
gay.

Pop Goes the Weasel

A penny for a ball of thread,
Another for a needle.
That's the way the money goes;
   Pop goes the Weasel!

All around the cobbler's bench
The monkey chased the people;
The donkey thought 'twas all in fun.
   Pop goes the Weasel!

Queen Victoria's very sick;
Napoleon's got the measles;
Sally's got the whooping cough;
   Pop goes the Weasel!

Of all the dances ever planned,
To fling the heel and fly the hand,
There's none that moves so gay and
   grand
   As Pop goes the Weasel!

A penny for a ball of thread,
Another for a needle.
That's the way the money goes;
   Pop goes the Weasel!

Taking Off

The airplane taxis down the field
And heads into the breeze,
It lifts its wheels above the ground,
It skims above the trees,
It rises high and higher
Away up toward the sun,
It's just a speck against the sky
— And now it's gone!

Daffadowndilly

Daffadowndilly
  Has come up to town,
In a yellow petticoat
  And a green gown.

Mother Goose

Little Boy Blue

The little toy dog is covered with
   dust,
But sturdy and staunch he stands;
And the little toy soldier is red with
   rust,
And his musket moulds in his
   hands.
Time was when the little toy dog was
   new,
And the soldier was passing fair;
And that was the time when our
   Little Boy Blue
Kissed them and put them there.

"Now, don't you go till I come," he
   said,
"And don't you make any noise!"
So, toddling off to his trundle-bed,
He dreamt of the pretty toys;
And, as he was dreaming, an angel
   song
Awakened our Little Boy Blue —
Oh! the years are many, the years are
   long,
But the little toy friends are true.

Ay, faithful to Little Boy Blue they
   stand,
Each in the same old place.
Awaiting the touch of a little hand,
The smile of a little face;
And they wonder, as waiting the
   long years through
In the dust of that little chair,
What has become of our Little Boy
   Blue,
Since he kissed them and put them
   there.

Eugene Field

Of Giving

Not what you Get, but what you
   Give
Is that which proves your Right to
   Live.

Arthur Guiterman

The Monkeys and the Crocodile

Five little monkeys
   Swinging from a tree;
Leaving Uncle Crocodile,
   Merry as can be.
Swinging high, swinging low,
   Swinging left and right:
"Dear Uncle Crocodile,
   Come and take a bite!"

Five little monkeys
   Swinging in the air;
Heads up, tails up,
   Little do they care.
Swinging up, swinging down,
   Swinging far and near:
"Poor Uncle Crocodile,
   Aren't you hungry, dear?"

Four little monkeys
   Sitting in a tree;
Heads down, tails down,
   Dreary as can be.
Weeping loud, weeping low,
   Crying to each other:
"Wicked Uncle Crocodile,
   To gobble up our brother!"

Laura E. Richards

Day-Dreamer

Too much thought:
Too little wrought.

*Adapted from the German by
Louis Untermeyer*

Clementine

In a cavern, in a canyon,
Excavating for a mine,
Dwelt a miner, forty-niner,
And his daughter Clementine.

Light she was and like a fairy,
And her shoes were number nine,
Herring boxes, without topses
Sandals were for Clementine.

Drove she ducklings to the water,
Every morning, just at nine,
Hit her foot against a splinter,
Fell into the foaming brine.

Ruby lips above the water,
Blowing bubbles soft and fine,
Alas for me! I was no swimmer
So I lost my Clementine.

Oh, my darling, oh, my darling,
Oh, my darling Clementine,
You are lost and gone forever,
Dreadful sorry, Clementine.

Under the greenwood tree
Who loves to lie with me,
And turn his merry note
Unto the sweet bird's throat,
Come hither, come hither, come
   hither:
Here shall he see
No enemy
But winter and rough weather.

William Shakespeare

Little Lost Pup

He was lost! — not a shade of doubt
    of that;
For he never barked at a slinking cat,
But stood in the square where the
    wind blew raw
With a drooping ear and a trembling
    paw
And a mournful look in his pleading
    eye
And a plaintive sniff at the passer-by
That begged as plain as a tongue
    could sue,
"O Mister! please may I follow you?"
A lorn wee waif of a tawny brown
Adrift in the roar of a heedless town.
Oh, the saddest of sights in a world
    of sin
Is a little lost pup with his tail tucked
    in!

Now he shares my board and he
    owns my bed,
And he fairly shouts when he hears
    my tread;
Then, if things go wrong, as they
    sometimes do,
He asserts his right to assuage my
    woes
With a warm, red tongue and a nice,
    cold nose
And a silky head on my arm or knee
And a paw as soft as a paw can be.

When we rove the woods for a
    league about
He's as full of pranks as a school let
    out;
For he romps and frisks like a three
    month's colt,
And he runs me down like a
    thunderbolt.
Oh, the blithest of sights in the
    world so fair
Is a gay little pup with his tail in the
    air!

Arthur Guiterman

Fairest Lord Jesus

Fairest Lord Jesus,
    Ruler of all nature,
Son of God and Son of Man!
    Thee will I cherish, thee will I
        honor,
Thou, my soul's glory, joy, and
    crown.

Fair are the meadows,
    Fair are the woodlands,
Robed in the blooming garb of
    spring:
    Jesus is fairer, Jesus is purer,
Who makes the woeful heart to sing.

Fair is the sunshine,
    Fair is the moonlight,
And all the twinkling, starry host:
    Jesus shines brighter, Jesus shines
        purer,
Than all the angels heaven can boast.

The Charge of the Light Brigade

Half a league, half a league,
    Half a league onward,
All in the valley of Death
    Rode the six hundred.
'Forward, the Light Brigade!
Charge for the guns!' he said:
Into the valley of Death
    Rode the six hundred.

'Forward, the Light Brigade!'
Was there a man dismayed?
Not though the soldier knew
    Some one had blundered:
Theirs not to make reply,
Theirs not to reason why,
Theirs but to do and die:
Into the valley of Death
    Rode the six hundred.

Cannon to right of them,
Cannon to left of them,
Cannon in front of them
  Volleyed and thundered;
Stormed at with shot and shell,
Boldly they rode and well,
Into the jaws of Death,
Into the mouth of Hell
  Rode the six hundred.

Flashed all their sabres bare,
Flashed as they turned in air
Sabring the gunners there,
Charging an army, while
  All the world wondered:
Plunged in the battery-smoke
Right through the line they broke;
Cossack and Russian
Reeled from the sabre-stroke
  Shattered and sundered.
Then they rode back, but not —
  Not the six hundred.

Cannon to right of them,
Cannon to left of them,
Cannon behind them
  Volleyed and thundered;
Stormed at with shot and shell,
While horse and hero fell,
They that had fought so well
Came through the jaws of Death,
Back from the mouth of Hell,
All that was left of them,
  Left of six hundred.

When can their glory fade?
O the wild charge they made!
  All the world wondered.
Honour the charge they made!
Honour the Light Brigade,
  Noble six hundred!

Alfred Tennyson

Oh, what a tangled web we weave,
When first we practice to deceive!

Walter Scott
(from Marmion)

A stitch in time saves nine.

Energy will do anything that can be
done in this world.

Johann Wolfgang von Goethe

Wealth is not his that has it, but his
that enjoys it.

Benjamin Franklin

Originality is simply a pair of fresh
eyes.

T. W. Higginson

Temperance and labor are the two
best physicians.

Rousseau

Genius is 90 percent perspiration, 10
percent inspiration.

Nothing dries sooner than a tear.

Truth never hurts the teller.

Elizabeth Barrett Browning

An apple a day
Will keep the doctor away.

When pleasant work is mixed with
    play,
It makes a very happy day.

I mean to make myself a man,
and if I succeed in that,
I shall succeed in everything else.

James A. Garfield

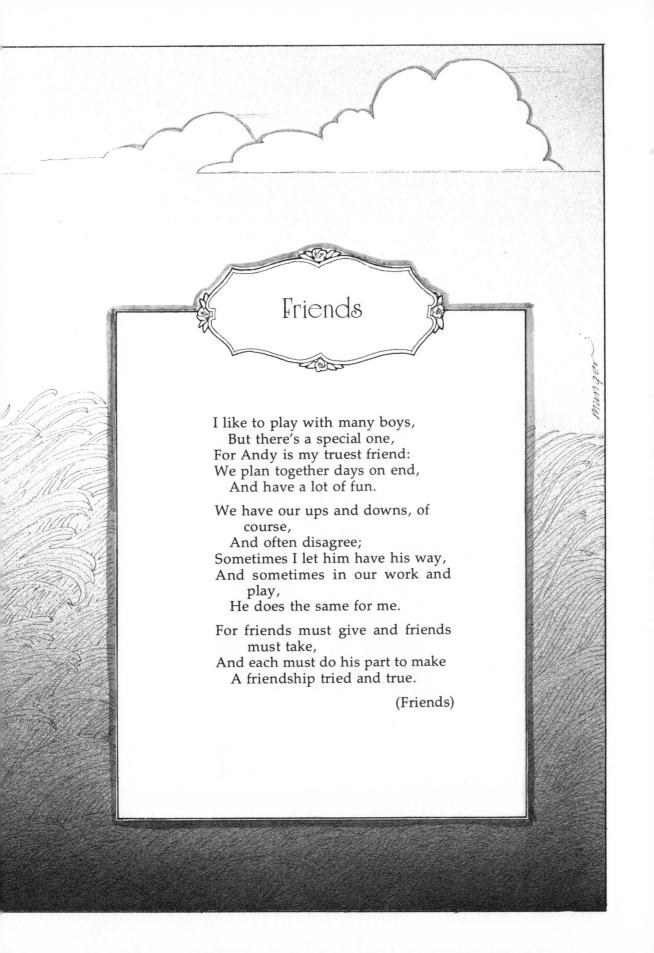

Friends

I like to play with many boys,
  But there's a special one,
For Andy is my truest friend:
We plan together days on end,
  And have a lot of fun.

We have our ups and downs, of
    course,
  And often disagree;
Sometimes I let him have his way,
And sometimes in our work and
    play,
  He does the same for me.

For friends must give and friends
    must take,
And each must do his part to make
  A friendship tried and true.

(Friends)

The Sandpiper

Across the narrow beach we flit,
One little sandpiper and I,
And fast I gather, bit by bit,
The scattered driftwood bleached
    and dry.
The wild waves reach their hands for
    it,
The wild wind raves, the tide runs
    high,
As up and down the beach we flit —
One little sandpiper and I.

Above our heads the sullen clouds
Scud black and swift across the sky;
Like silent ghosts in misty shrouds
Stand out the white lighthouses
    high.
Almost as far as eye can reach
I see the close-reefed vessels fly,
As fast we flit along the beach —
One little sandpiper and I.

I watch him as he skims along,
Uttering his sweet and mournful
    cry.
He starts not at my fitful song,
Or flash of fluttering drapery.
He has no thought of any wrong;
He scans me with a fearless eye:
Staunch friends are we, well tried
    and strong,
The little sandpiper and I.

Comrade, where wilt thou be
    tonight
When the loosed storm breaks
    furiously?
My driftwood fire will burn so
    bright!
To what warm shelter canst thou fly?
I do not fear for thee, though wroth
The tempest rushes through the sky:
For are we not God's children both,
Thou, little sandpiper, and I?

Celia Thaxter

Growing Friendship

Friendship is like a garden of
    flowers, fine and rare;
It cannot reach perfection except
    through loving care;
Then, new and lovely blossoms with
    each new day appear —
For Friendship, like a garden, grows
    in beauty year by year.

There's happiness in little things,
There's joy in passing pleasure;
But friendships are, from year to
    year,
The best of all life's treasure.

It's a Funny Thing but True

It's a funny thing, but true,
The folks you don't like, don't like
    you.
I don't know why this should be so,
But just the same I always know
That when I'm sour, friends are few;
When I'm friendly, folks are, too.
I sometimes get up in the morn,
Awishin' I was never born,
And then I make cross remarks, a
    few,
And then my family wishes, too,
That I had gone some other place,
But then I change my little tune,
And sing and smile,
And then the folks around me sing
    and smile.
I guess 'twas catching all the while.
It's a funny thing, but true,
The folks you like, they sure like
    you.

86

Jenny White and Johnny Black

Jenny White and Johnny Black
  Went out for a walk.
Jenny found wild strawberries,
  And John a lump of chalk.

Jenny White and Johnny Black
  Clambered up a hill.
Jenny heard a willow-wren,
  And John a workman's drill.

Jenny White and Johnny Black
  Wandered by the dike.
Jenny smelt the meadow sweet,
  And John a motor-bike.

Jenny White and Johnny Black
  Turned into a lane.
Jenny saw the moon by day,
  And Johnny saw a train.

Jenny White and Johnny Black
  Walked into a storm.
Each felt for the other's hand
  And found it nice and warm.

Eleanor Farjeon

Friends

How good to lie a little while
  And look up through the tree —
The Sky is like a kind big smile
  Bent sweetly over me.

The Sunshine flickers through the
    lace
  Of leaves above my head,
And kisses me upon the face
  Like Mother, before bed.

The Wind comes stealing o'er the
    grass
  To whisper pretty things;
And though I cannot see him pass,
  I feel his careful wings.

So many gentle Friends are near
  Whom one can scarcely see,
A child should never feel a fear,
  Wherever he may be.

Abbie Farwell Brown

Jesus, Friend of Little Children

Jesus, friend of little children,
Be a friend to me;
Take my hand and ever keep me
Close to Thee.

Teach me how to grow in goodness
Daily as I grow;
Thou has been a child and surely
Thou dost know.

Fill me with Thy gentle meekness,
Make my heart like Thine;
Like an altar lamp then let me
Burn and shine.

Step by step, O lead me onward,
Upward into youth;
Wiser, stronger still, becoming,
In Thy truth.

Walter J. Mathams

A Little Word

A little word in kindness spoken,
    A motion or a tear,
Has often healed the heart that's
    broken,
And made a friend sincere.

Daniel Clement Colesworthy

No one is too small to be able to help
a friend.

A true friend is the best possession.

Talk not of wasted affection,
    affection never was wasted;
If it enrich not the heart of another,
    its waters, returning
Back to their springs, like the rain,
    shall fill them full of refreshment;
That which the fountain sends forth
        returns
    again to the fountain.

Henry Wadsworth Longfellow
(from Evangeline)

The only safe
And sure way
To destroy an enemy:
Make him your friend.

A friend is a person
    who likes you
    for what you are
    in spite of your faults.

In Gratitude for Friends

I thank You, God in Heaven, for
        friends.
When morning wakes, when
        daytime ends.
    I have the consciousness
Of loving hands that touch my own,
Of tender glance and gentle tone,
    Of thoughts that cheer and bless!
If sorrow comes to me I know
That friends will walk the way I go,
    And, as the shadows fall,
I know that I will raise my eyes
And see — ah, hope that never
        dies! —
    The dearest Friend of All.

Margaret E. Sangster

Make Me Worthy of My Friends

It is my joy in life to find
    At every turning of the road
The strong arms of a comrade kind
    To help me onward with my load.
And since I have no gold to give
    And love alone can make amends,
My only prayer is, "While I live,
    God, make me worthy of my
        friends!"

The Arrow and the Song

I shot an arrow into the air,
It fell to earth, I knew not where;
For, so swiftly it flew, the sight
Could not follow it in its flight.

I breathed a song into the air,
It fell to earth, I knew not where;
For who has sight so keen and
     strong,
That it can follow the flight of song?

Long, long afterward, in an oak
I found the arrow, still unbroke;
And the song, from beginning to
     end,
I found again in the heart of a friend.

Henry Wadsworth Longfellow

Fun and Nonsense

Bibbily Boo, the king so free,
He used to drink the Mango tea.
Mango tea and coffee, too,
He drank them both till his nose
   turned blue.

Wollypotump, the queen so high,
She used to eat the Gumbo pie.
Gumbo pie and Gumbo cake,
She ate them both till her teeth did
   break.

Bibbily Boo and Wollypotump,
Each called the other a greedy
   frump.
And when these terrible words were
   said,
They sat and cried till they both were
   dead.

(Bibbily Boo and Wollypotump)
Laura E. Richards

There Was an Old Man With a Beard

There was an Old Man with a beard,
Who said, "It is just as I feared! —
   Two Owls and a Hen,
   Four Larks and a Wren,
Have all built their nests in my
    beard."

                Edward Lear

Antonio

Antonio, Antonio,
Was tired of living alonio.
   He thought he would woo
   Miss Lissamy Lu,
Miss Lissamy Lucy Molino.

Antonio, Antonio,
Rode off on his polo-ponio.
   He found the fair maid
   In a bowery shade,
A-sitting and knitting alonio.

Antonio, Antonio,
Said, "If you will be my ownio,
   I'll love you true,
   And I'll buy for you,
An icery creamery conio!"

"Oh, nonio, Antonio!
You're far too bleak and bonio!
   And all that I wish,
   You singular fish,
Is that you will quickly begonio."

Antonio, Antonio,
He uttered a dismal moanio;
   Then ran off and hid
   (Or I'm told that he did)
In the Antarctical Zonio.

                Laura E. Richards

Roses are red,
Violets are blue,
I copied your paper,
And I flunked too.

Foolish Flowers

We've Foxgloves in our garden;
   How careless they must be
To leave their gloves out hanging
   Where every one can see!

And Bachelors leave their Buttons
   In the same careless way;
If I should do the same with mine,
   What would Mother say?

We've lots of Larkspurs in the
    yard —
   Larks only fly and sing —
Birds surely don't need spurs
    because
   They don't ride anything!

And as for Johnny-Jump-Ups —
   I saw a hornet light
On one of them the other day;
   He didn't jump a mite!

Rupert Sargent Holland

There Were Three Ghostesses

There were three ghostesses
Sitting on postesses
Eating buttered toastesses
And greasing their fistesses
Right up to their wristesses.
Weren't they beastesses
To make such feastesses?

Oh, the Funniest Thing

Oh, the funniest thing
   I've ever seen
Was a tomcat sewing
   On a sewing machine.
Oh, the sewing machine
   Got running too slow,
And it took seven stitches
   In the tomcat's toe.

Five Little Squirrels

Five little squirrels sat up in a tree.
The first one said, "What do I see?"
The second one said, "A man with a
    gun."
The third one said, "Then we'd
    better run."
The fourth one said, "Let's hide in
    the shade."
The fifth one said, "I'm not afraid."
Then BANG went the gun,
And how they did run.

A Tutor Who Tooted the Flute

A Tutor who tooted the flute
Tried to teach two young tooters to
    toot;
    Said the two to the Tutor,
    "Is it harder to toot, or
To tutor two tooters to toot?"

"The time has come," the Walrus
    said,
    "To talk of many things:
Of shoes — and ships — and
    sealing-wax —
Of cabbages — and kings —
And why the sea is boiling hot —
    And whether pigs have wings."

Lewis Carroll

The Twins

In form and feature, face and limb,
    I grew so like my brother,
That folks got taking me for him,
    And each for one another.
It puzzled all our kith and kin,
    It reached an awful pitch;
For one of us was born a twin,
    Yet not a soul knew which.

One day (to make the matter worse),
    Before our names were fixed,
As we were being washed by nurse
    We got completely mixed;
And thus, you see, by Fate's decree,
    (Or rather nurse's whim),
My brother John got christened *me*,
    And I got christened *him*.

This fatal likeness even dogg'd
    My footsteps when at school,
And I was always getting flogg'd,
    For John turned out a fool.
I put this question hopelessly
    To everyone I knew —
What *would* you do, if you were me,
    To prove that you were *you*?

Our close resemblance turned the
    tide
    Of my domestic life;
For somehow my intended bride
    Became my brother's wife.
In short, year after year the same
    Absurd mistake went on;
And when I died — the neighbors
    came
    And buried brother John!

Henry S. Leigh

Inky, dinky spider
Climbed up the waterspout;
Down came the rain
And washed the spider out;
Up came the sun
And drove away the rain;
Inky, dinky spider climbed up the
    spout again.

Poor Old Lady

Poor old lady, she swallowed a fly.
I don't know why she swallowed a
    fly.
Poor old lady, I think she'll die.

Poor old lady, she swallowed a
    spider,
It squirmed and wriggled and
    turned inside her.
She swallowed the spider to catch
    the fly.
I don't know why she swallowed a
    fly.
Poor old lady, I think she'll die.

Poor old lady, she swallowed a bird.
How absurd! She swallowed a bird.
She swallowed the bird to catch the
    spider,
She swallowed the spider to catch
    the fly.
I don't know why she swallowed a
    fly.
Poor old lady, I think she'll die.

Poor old lady, she swallowed a cat.
Think of that! She swallowed a cat.
She swallowed the cat to catch the
    bird,
She swallowed the bird to catch the
    spider,
She swallowed the spider to catch
    the fly.
I don't know why she swallowed a
    fly.
Poor old lady, I think she'll die.

Poor old lady, she swallowed a dog.
She went the whole hog when she
    swallowed the dog.
She swallowed the dog to catch the
    cat,
She swallowed the cat to catch the
    bird,
She swallowed the bird to catch the
    spider,
She swallowed the spider to catch
    the fly.
I don't know why she swallowed a
    fly.
Poor old lady, I think she'll die.

Poor old lady, she swallowed a cow.
I don't know how she swallowed a
    cow.
She swallowed a cow to catch the
    dog,
She swallowed the dog to catch the
    cat,
She swallowed the cat to catch the
    bird,
She swallowed the bird to catch the
    spider,
She swallowed the spider to catch
    the fly.
I don't know why she swallowed a
    fly.
Poor old lady, I think she'll die.

Poor old lady, she swallowed a
    horse.
She died, of course.

(attributed to Pamela Smith)

The Poor Unfortunate Hottentot

A poor unfortunate Hottentot
He was not content with his
    lottentot;
    Quoth he, "For my dinner,
    As I am a sinner,
There's nothing to put in the
    pottentot!"

This poor unfortunate Hottentot
Said, "Yield to starvation I'll
    nottentot;
  I'll see if I can't elope
  With a young antelope —
One who'll enjoy being shottentot."

This poor unfortunate Hottentot
His bow and his arrows he
    gottentot;
  And being stout-hearted,
  At once he departed,
And struck through the Bush at a
    trottentot.

This poor unfortunate Hottentot,
Was not many miles from his
    cottentot,
  When he chanced to set eyes on
  A snake that was pison,
A-tying itself in a knottentot.

This poor unfortunate Hottentot
Remarked, "This for me is not
    spottentot!
  I'd better be going;
  There's really no knowing;
I might on his view be a blottentot."

This poor unfortunate Hottentot,
Was turning to fly to his grottentot,
  When a lioness met him,
  And suddenly ate him,
As penny's engulfed by the
    slottentot.

Moral

This poor unfortunate Hottentot,
Had better have borne with his
    lottentot.
  A simple banana
  Had staved off Nirvana;
But what had become of my
    plottentot?

Laura E. Richards

Some Fishy Nonsense

Timothy Tiggs and Tomothy Toggs,
They both went a-fishing for
    pollothywogs;
  They both went a-fishing
  Because they were wishing
To see how the creatures would turn
    into frogs.

Timothy Tiggs and Tomothy Toggs,
They both got stuck in the
    bogothybogs;
  They caught a small minnow
  And said 'twas a sin oh!
That things with no legs should
    pretend to be frogs.

Laura E. Richards

Fifty Cents

I asked my mother for fifty cents
To see the elephant jump the fence.

He jumped so high,
He reached the sky.

He never came back
'Til the Fourth of July.

Fun

I love to see a lobster laugh
Or see a turtle wiggle
Or poke a hippopotamus
And see the monster giggle,
Or even stand around at night
And watch the mountains wriggle.

Leroy F. Jackson

There was a young lady of Riga,
Who rode with a smile on a tiger;
  They returned from the ride
  With the lady inside,
And the smile on the face of the
    tiger.

There was a young lady of Lynn,
Who was so uncommonly thin,
  That when she essayed
  To drink lemonade,
She slipped through the straw and
    fell in.

The Purple Cow

I never saw a purple cow
I never hope to see one,
But I can tell you anyhow,
I'd rather see than be one!

Gelett Burgess

A cheerful old bear at the zoo
Could always find something to do.
  When it bored him, you know,
  To walk to and fro,
He reversed it and walked fro and to.

On Leslie Moore

Here lies what's left
Of Leslie Moore
  No Les
  No More

The Ostrich Is a Silly Bird

The ostrich is a silly bird,
  With scarcely any mind.
He often runs so very fast,
  He leaves himself behind.

And when he gets there, has to stand
  And hang about till night,
Without a blessed thing to do
  Until he comes in sight.

Mary E. Wilkins Freeman

State Quiz

What did Delaware?
  She wore her New Jersey.
Where has Oregon?
  He's taking Oklahoma.
What does Iowa? Idaho
  She hoes the Maryland.
How did Connecticut?
  She used the New Hampshire.
What does Mississippi?
  She sips her Old Virginia.
How does Florida?
  She died of Missouri.
How did Wisconsin?
  He stole the Nebraska.
What did Tennessee?
  He saw what Arkansas.
What did Massachusetts?
  He chewed his Old Kentucky.

Theophilus Thistledown

Theophilus Thistledown, the
    successful thistle sifter,
In sifting a sieve of unsifted thistles,
Thrust three thousand thistles
Through the thick of his thumb.
If then, Theophilus Thistledown,
    the successful thistle sifter,
In sifting a sieve of unsifted thistles,
Thrust three thousand thistles
Through the thick of his thumb,
See that thou, in sifting a sieve of
    unsifted thistles,
Do not get the unsifted thistles stuck
    in thy tongue.

Jaybird

Jaybird a-sitting on a hickory limb;
    He winked at me and I winked
    at him.
I picked up a rock and hit him on the
    chin.
Says he, "Young feller, don't you do
    that again!"

A Tragic Story

There lived a sage in days of yore,
And he a handsome pigtail wore;
But wondered much and sorrowed
    more,
Because it hung behind him.

He mused upon this curious case,
And swore he'd change the pigtail's
    place,
And have it hanging at his face,
Not dangling there behind him.

Says he, "The mystery I've found —
I'll turn me round," — he turned him
    round;
But still it hung behind him.
Then round and round, and out and
    in,
All day the puzzled sage did spin;
In vain — it mattered not a pin —
The pigtail hung behind him.

And right and left, and round about,
And up and down, and in and out,
He turned; but still the pigtail stout
Hung steadily behind him.

And though his efforts never slack,
And though he twist and twirl and
    tack,
Alas! still faithful to his back,
The pigtail hangs behind him.

William Makepeace Thackeray 1817 - 1893

Ashes to ashes
Dust to dust,
Oil those brains
Before they rust.

You can lead a horse to water,
But you cannot make him drink.
You can send a fool to college,
But you cannot make him think.

A Flea and a Fly in a Flue

A flea and a fly in a flue
Were imprisoned, so what could
    they do?
  Said the fly, "Let us flee,"
  Said the flea, "Let us fly,"
So they flew through a flaw in the
    flue.

On a mule you find two feet behind,
Two feet you find before;
You stand behind before you find
What the two behind be for.

Peas

I always eat peas with honey,
I've done it all my life,
They do taste kind of funny,
But it keeps them on my knife.

The noble Duke of York,
He had ten thousand men,
He marched them up to the top of the
        hill,
And he marched them down again.
And when they were up, they were
        up,
And when they were down, they
        were down,
And when they were only half way
        up,
    They were neither up nor down.

A young theologian named Fiddle
Refused to accept his degree.
"For," said he, " 'tis enough to be
        Fiddle,
Without being Fiddle, D.D."

Buttons

The front ones I can button fine
The side ones keep me busy
But buttons all the way behind
I hunt until I'm dizzy!

Riddles

How can you tell that the elephant is a traveler?

Because he always carries his trunk.

When is an ear of corn like a baby?

When it's in the crib.

Why does a king never carry an umbrella?

He is used to reign (rain).

Why does a skinny man go to the beach?

To look for mussels (muscles).

What has a tongue and can't talk?

A shoe.

What tool grows sharper with use?

The tongue.

What is it that can be broken without being dropped or hit?

A promise.

What is the best way to keep fish from smelling?

Cut off their noses.

Ten cats were in a boat. One jumped out. How many were left?

None. They were copycats.

Why isn't your nose twelve inches long?

Because it would be a foot.

What do you call a man who is always wiring for money?

An electrician.

Which side of an apple pie is the left side?

The part that isn't eaten.

Which is the strongest day of the week?

Sunday, because all the rest are week (weak) days.

Three men fell into the lake, but only two men got their hair wet. Why?

One was bald.

How can you get into a locked cemetery at night?

Use a skeleton key.

What two animals go with you everywhere?

Your calves.

What is everybody in the world doing at the same time?

Growing older.

What has a foot at each end and one in the middle?

A yardstick.

What is worse than a centipede with sore feet?

A giraffe with a sore throat.

Why is it cheap to feed a giraffe?

He makes a little food go a long way.

What is it you have that everyone else uses more than you do?

Your name.

What is black and white and read all over?

A newspaper.

What is the surest way to double your dollar?

Fold it.

Why is a fraidycat like a leaky faucet?

They both keep running.

When is a man obliged to keep his word?

When no one else will take it.

What can speak every language in the world?

An echo.

What do cats have that children want?

Kittens.

What animal took the most baggage into Noah's ark?

The elephant. He took his trunk.

What animals took the least baggage into Noah's ark?

The fox and the rooster. They only had a brush and a comb between them.

Where was Solomon's temple?

On the side of his head.

What starts with T, ends with T, and is full of T?

A teapot.

Who was the most successful doctor in the Bible?

Job, because he had the most patience (patients).

Who was the straightest man in the Bible?

Joseph, because King Pharaoh made a ruler out of him.

What can't you name without breaking it?

Silence.

Growing Up

Blessings on thee, little man,
Barefoot boy, with cheek of tan!
With thy turned-up pantaloons,
And thy merry whistled tunes;
With thy red lip, redder still
Kissed by strawberries on the hill;
With the sunshine on thy face,
Through thy torn brim's jaunty
        grace;
From my heart I give thee joy, —
I was once a barefoot boy!
Prince thou art, — the grown-up
        man
Only is republican.
Let the million-dollared ride!
Barefoot, trudging at his side,
Thou hast more than he can buy
In the reach of ear and eye, —
Outward sunshine, inward joy:
Blessings on thee, barefoot boy!

Oh, for boyhood's painless play,
Sleep that wakes in laughing day,
Health that mocks the doctor's rules,
Knowledge never learned of schools,
Of the wild bee's morning chase,
Of the wild flower's time and place,
Flight of fowl and habitude
Of the tenants of the wood;
How the tortoise bears his shell,
How the woodchuck digs his cell,
And the ground-mole sinks his well;
How the robin feeds her young,
How the oriole's nest is hung;
Where the whitest lilies blow,
Where the freshest berries grow,
Where the ground-nut trails its vine,
Where the wood-grape's clusters
        shine;
Of the black wasp's cunning way,
Mason of his walls of clay,
And the architectural plans
Of gray hornet artisans!
For, eschewing books and tasks,
Nature answers all he asks;
Hand in hand with her he walks,
Face to face with her he talks,
Part and parcel of her joy, —
Blessings on the barefoot boy!

Oh, for boyhood's time of June,
Crowding years in one brief moon,
When all things I heard or saw,
Me, their master, waited for.
I was rich in flowers and trees,
Humming birds and honey-bees;
For my sport the squirrel played,
Plied the snouted mole his spade;
For my taste the blackberry cone
Purpled over hedge and stone;
Laughed the brook for my delight
Through the day and through the
        night, —
Whispering at the garden wall,
Talked with me from fall to fall;
Mine the sand-rimmed pickerel
        pond,
Mine the walnut slopes beyond,
Mine, on bending orchard trees,
Apples of Hesperides!
Still as my horizon grew,
Larger grew my riches too;
All the world I saw or knew

Seemed a complex Chinese toy,
Fashioned for a barefoot boy!

Oh, for festal dainties spread,
Like my bowl of milk and bread;
Pewter spoon and bowl of wood,
On the door-stone, gray and rude!
O'er me, like a regal tent,
Cloudy-ribbed, the sunset bent,
Purple-curtained, fringed with gold,
Looped in many a wind-swung fold;
While for music came the play
Of the pied frogs' orchestra;
And, to light the noisy choir,
Lit the fly his lamp of fire.
I was monarch: pomp and joy
Waited on the barefoot boy!

Cheerily, then, my little man,
Live and laugh, as boyhood can!
Though the flinty slopes be hard,
Stubble-speared the new-mown
        sward,
Every morn shall lead thee through
Fresh baptisms of the dew;
Every evening from thy feet
Shall the cool wind kiss the heat:
All too soon these feet must hide
In the prison cells of pride,
Lose the freedom of the sod,
Like a colt's for work be shod,
Made to tread the mills of toil,
Up and down in ceaseless moil:
Happy if their track be found
Never on forbidden ground;
Happy if they sink not in
Quick and treacherous sands of sin.
Ah! that thou couldst know thy joy,
Ere it passes, barefoot boy!

(The Barefoot Boy)
John Greenleaf Whittier

Patience is a virtue,
    virtue is a grace;
Both put together
    make a pretty face.

A Boy's Song

Where the pools are bright and
    deep,
Where the gray trout lies asleep,
Up the river, and over the lea,
That's the way for Billy and me.

Where the blackbird sings the latest,
Where the hawthorne blooms the
    sweetest,
Where the nestlings chirp and flee,
That's the way for Billy and me.

Where the mowers mow the
    cleanest,
Where the hay lies thick and
    greenest,
There to trace the homeward bee,
That's the way for Billy and me.

Where the hazel bank is steepest,
Where the shadow falls the deepest,
Where the clustering nuts fall free,
That's the way for Billy and me.

James Hogg

Decision

Golly, it's hard
To decide what to pick . . .
I sure do like lollipops,
They're fun to lick;
But look at those jawbreakers!
They last and last;
Gumdrops are better,
But go down too fast;
Can't get rock candy . . .
Mom says it's too hard;
Bubble gum comes
With a free baseball card;
That pink colored taffy
Is sure nice and chewy;
Might just get caramels,
They're not so gooey!
Golly, it's tough
To pick from so many.
Wish I had a dollar
Instead of a penny!

M. P. Flynn

The Winning of the TV West

When twilight comes to Prairie
    Street
On every TV channel,
The kids watch men with blazing
    guns
In jeans and checkered flannel.
Partner, the West is wild tonight —
There's going to be a battle
Between the sheriff's posse and
The gang that stole the cattle.
On every screen on Prairie Street
The sheriff roars his order:
"We've got to head those hombres
    off
Before they reach the border."
Clippoty-clop and bangity-bang
The lead flies left and right.
Paradise Valley is freed again
Until tomorrow night.
And all the kids on Prairie Street
Over and under ten
Can safely go to dinner now . . .
The West is won again.

John T. Alexander

Aren't You Glad

The world is made of days and
    nights,
of wind and rain and trees,
Of boys and girls and grownups,
    who grow in families.
I'll tell you about these.

Little girls have soft hair
    and necklaces and lace,
        daintiness and dolls
And sweetness in their face.
    Oh, dance and swirl, dance and
        twirl,
        ballet toes, little girl.

Little boys are rougher,
    with bikes and balls and blocks;
Little boys are tougher
    in corduroys and socks.
Please and tease and lots of noise,
That's the way of little boys.

Little girls who grow up
    are mothers, aunts, and
        grandmas;
Little boys who grow up
    are fathers, friends, and
        grandpas.
    All of these make families.

Little cats are furriness,
Green eyes that glow,
    and purriness.
Slither and prowl, skit and skat
Through the garden, little cat.

Little dogs are woofs and barks,
    pink tongues and wagging tails;
Little dogs are cold, wet noses
    and paws with scratchy nails.
Loppety log, joggety jog,
Your paws go pattery, little dog.

Little girls and little boys,
Little cats and dogs —
    all of these
    make families,
And families live in houses,
    made of windows, doors, and
        stairs,
    of beds and books and bathtubs,
    of tables and of chairs.

Roots and branches and leaves
And the rustling of wind make trees;
    sunny trees rustle and sigh,
    glimmer and shimmer against the
        sky.
The sun outside means time to play
    in its warmth and light-gold light;
But darkness outside and the moon
    up high,
The bed turned down and stars to
    sleep by come at night.

The world is the sun and its light-
    gold light
The bed turned down and the stars
    at night,
The roots and the branches and
    wind in the leaves,
The dogs and the cats and the
    families.
    Oh, aren't you glad
    you're part of these?

Charlotte Zolotow

Mother of the House

Strength and dignity are her
    clothing,
    and she laughs at the time to
        come.
She opens her mouth to wisdom,
    and the teaching of kindness
        is on her tongue.
She looks well to the ways of her
    household,
    and does not eat the bread of
        idleness.
Her children rise up and call her
    blessed;
    her husband also, and he praises
        her:
"Many women have done
    excellently,
    but you surpass them all."

The Bible, Proverbs 31:25-29, RSV

Recipe

I can make a sandwich.
I can really cook.
I made up this recipe
That should be in a book:
Take a jar of peanut butter,
Give it a spread,
Until you have covered
A half a loaf of bread.
Pickles and pineapple,
Strawberry jam,
Salami and bologna
And half a pound of ham —
Pour some catsup on it.
Mix in the mustard well.
It will taste delicious,
If you don't mind the smell.

Bobbi Katz

Down in the Field

Down in the field
   Among tall grass
   and fever weeds that blow —
   I'd go.

Trees about
   And those beyond
   All seemed to know:
I'd put my schoolroom manners
   On the shelf
To play at being no one
   But myself.

M. P. Flynn

A Prayer for the Young and Lovely

Dear God, I keep praying
For the things I desire,
You tell me I am selfish
And "playing with fire" —
It is hard to believe
I am selfish and vain.
My desires seem so real
And my needs seem so sane,
And yet You are wiser
And Your vision is wide
And You look down on me
And You see deep inside,
You know it's so easy
To change and distort,
And things that are evil
Seem so harmless a sport —
Oh, teach me, dear God,
To not rush ahead
But to pray for Your guidance
And to trust You instead,
For You know what I need
And that I'm only a slave
To the things that I want
And desire and crave —
Oh, God, in Your mercy
Look down on me now
And see in my heart
That I love You somehow,
Although in my rashness,
Impatience and greed
I pray for the things
That I want and don't need —
And instead of a crown
Please send me a cross
And teach me to know
That all gain is but loss,
And show me the way
To joy without end,
With You as my Father,
Redeemer and Friend —
And send me the things
That are hardest to bear,
And keep me forever
Safe in Your care.

Helen Steiner Rice

At the Seaside

When I was down beside the sea
A wooden spade they gave to me
To dig the sandy shore.

My holes were empty like a cup.
In every hole the sea came up,
Till it could come no more.

Robert Louis Stevenson

How Pleasant Is Saturday Night

How pleasant is Saturday night,
When I've tried all the week to be
    good,
Not spoken a word that was bad
And obliged everyone that I could.

School Is Over

School is over,
    Oh, what fun!
Lessons finished,
    Play begun.
Who'll run fastest,
    You or I?
Who'll laugh loudest?
    Let us try.

Kate Greenaway

My Shadow

I have a little shadow that goes in
    and out with me,
And what can be the use of him is
    more than I can see.
He is very, very like me from the
    heels up to the head;
And I see him jump before me, when
    I jump into my bed.

The funniest thing about him is the
    way he likes to grow —
Not at all like proper children, which
    is always very slow;
For he sometimes shoots up taller
    like an India-rubber ball,
And he sometimes gets so little that
    there's none of him at all.

He hasn't got a notion of how chil-
    dren ought to play,
And can only make a fool of me in
    every sort of way.
He stays so close beside me, he's a
    coward you can see;
I'd think shame to stick to nursie as
    that shadow sticks to me!

One morning, very early, before the
    sun was up,
I rose and found the shining dew on
    every buttercup;
But my lazy little shadow, like an
    arrant sleepy-head,
Had stayed at home behind me and
    was fast asleep in bed.

Robert Louis Stevenson

My Aim

As I grow more and more each day,
I'll try to live the friendly way.
I'll try hard to say and do
Only what is kind and true.

Always it shall be my aim
To play fair in any game,
Keep myself alert but cool,
Try to live the Golden Rule.

Alexander Seymour

If

If you can keep your head when all
about you
    Are losing theirs and blaming it
on you;
If you can trust yourself when all
men doubt you,
    But make allowance for their
doubting too;
If you can wait and not be tired by
waiting,
    Or, being lied about, don't deal in
lies,
Or, being hated, don't give way to
hating,
    And yet don't look too good, nor
talk too wise;

If you can dream — and not make
dreams your master;
    If you can think — and not make
thoughts your aim;
If you can meet with triumph and
disaster
    And treat those two impostors just
the same;
If you can bear to hear the truth
you've spoken
    Twisted by knaves to make a trap
for fools,
Or watch the things you gave your
life to broken,
    And stoop and build 'em up with
worn-out tools;

If you can make one heap of all your
winnings
    And risk it on one turn of pitch-
and-toss,
And lose, and start again at your
beginnings
    And never breathe a word about
your loss;
If you can force your heart and nerve
and sinew
    To serve your turn long after they
are gone,
And so hold on when there is
nothing in you
    Except the Will which says to
them: "Hold on";

If you can talk with crowds and keep
your virtue,
    Or walk with kings — nor lose the
common touch;
If neither foes nor loving friends can
hurt you;
    If all men count with you, but
none too much;
If you can fill the unforgiving minute
    With six seconds' worth of
distance run —
Yours is the Earth and everything
that's in it,
    And — which is more — you'll be
a Man, my son!

Rudyard Kipling

Mr. Nobody

I know a funny little man,
    As quiet as a mouse,
Who does the mischief that is done
    In everybody's house!
There's no one ever sees his face,
    And yet we all agree
That every plate we break was
cracked
    By Mr. Nobody.

'Tis he who always tears our books,
    Who leaves the door ajar,
He pulls the buttons from our shirts,
    And scatters pins afar;
That speaking door will always
speak,
    For, prithee, don't you see,
We leave the oiling to be done
    By Mr. Nobody.

The fingermarks upon the door
    By none of us are made;
We never leave the blinds unclosed,
    To let the curtains fade.
The ink we never spill; the boots
    That lying round you see
Are not our boots — they all belong
    To Mr. Nobody.

There Was a Child Went Forth

There was a child went forth every
  day;
And the first object he looked upon,
  that object he became.
And that object became part of him
  for the day, or a certain part of
  the day, or for many years,
  or stretching cycles of years:
The early lilacs became part of this
  child. . . .
And the apple-trees covered with
  blossoms, and the fruit afterward, and wood-berries, and
  the commonest weeds by the
  road;
And the schoolmistress that passed
  on her way to the school. . . .

The blow, the quick loud word, the
  tight bargain, the crafty lure,
The family usages, the language, the
  company, the furniture — the
  yearning and swelling heart.
The doubts of day-time and the
  doubts of night-time — the
  curious whether and how,
Whether that which appears is so, or
  is it all flashes and specks?
Men and women crowding fast in
  the streets — if they are not
  flashes and specks, what are
  they?

These became part of that child who
  went forth every day,
and who now goes, and will always
  go forth every day.

Walt Whitman

Me

As long as I live
I shall always be
My Self — and no other,
Just me.

Like a tree.

Like a willow or elder,
An aspen, a thorn,
Or a cypress forlorn.

Like a flower,
For its hour,
A primrose, a pink,
Or a violet —
Sunned by the sun
And with dewdrops wet.

Always just me.

Walter de la Mare

He Was One of Us

He was born as little children are
  and lived as children do,
So remember that the Saviour
  was once a child like you,
And remember that He lived on
  earth
  in the midst of sinful men,
And the problems of the present
  existed even then;
He was ridiculed and laughed at
  in the same heartbreaking way
That we who fight for justice
  are ridiculed today;
He was tempted . . . He was
  hungry . . .
  He was lonely . . . He was sad . . .
There's no sorrowful experience
  that the Saviour has not had;
And in the end He was betrayed
  and even crucified,
For He was truly "One of Us" —
  He lived on earth and died;
So do not heed the skeptics
  who are often heard to say:
"What does God up in heaven
  know of things we face today" . . .

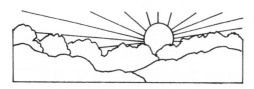

For, our Father up in heaven
   is very much aware
Of our failures and shortcomings
   and the burdens that we bear;
So whenever you are troubled
   put your problems in God's hand
For He has faced all problems
   and He will understand.

Helen Steiner Rice

Animal Crackers

Animal crackers, and cocoa to drink,
That is the finest of suppers, I think;
When I'm grown up and can have
   what I please
I think I shall always insist upon
   these.

What do *you* choose when you're
   offered a treat?
When Mother says, "What would
   you like best to eat?"
Is it waffles and syrup, or cinnamon
   toast?
It's cocoa and animals that *I* love
   most!

The kitchen's the cosiest place that I
   know:
The kettle is singing, the stove is
   aglow,
And there in the twilight, how jolly
   to see
The cocoa and animals waiting for
   me.

Daddy and Mother dine later in
   state,
With Mary to cook for them, Susan
   to wait;
But they don't have nearly as much
   fun as I
Who eat in the kitchen with Nurse
   standing by;
And Daddy once said he would like
   to be me
Having cocoa and animals once
   more for tea!

Christopher Morley

Lullaby

Sweet and low, sweet and low,
   Wind of the western sea,
Low, low, breathe and blow,
   Wind of the western sea!
Over the rolling waters go,
Come from the dying moon, and
   blow,
   Blow him again to me;
While my little one, while my pretty
   one, sleeps.

Sleep and rest, sleep and rest,
   Father will come to thee soon;
Rest, rest, on mother's breast,
   Father will come to thee soon;
Father will come to his bird in the
   nest;
Silver sails all out of the west
   Under the silver moon:
Sleep, my little one, sleep, my pretty
   one, sleep.

Alfred Tennyson
(from The Princess)

Little

I am the sister of him
And he is my brother.
He is too little for us
To talk to each other.

So every morning I show him
My doll and my book;
But every morning he still is
Too little to look.

Dorothy Aldis

The Little Elf

I met a little Elf-man, once,
 Down where the lilies blow.
I asked him why he was so small
 And why he didn't grow.

He slightly frowned, and with his
 eye
 He looked me through and
 through.
"I'm quite as big for me," said he,
 "As you are big for you."

John Kendrick Bangs

Two in Bed

When my brother Tommy
 Sleeps in bed with me,
 He doubles up
 And makes
 himself
 exactly
 like
 a
 V
And 'cause the bed is not so wide,
A part of him is on my side.

A. B. Ross

I am glad I'm who I am;
I like to be myself.
Even when I do the wrong thing,
I know I am the right person.

Jessie Orton Jones
(VIII from Secrets)

Only One Mother

Hundreds of stars in the pretty sky,
 Hundreds of shells on the shore
 together,
Hundreds of birds that go singing
 by,
 Hundreds of lambs in the sunny
 weather.

Hundreds of dewdrops to greet the
 dawn,
 Hundreds of bees in the purple
 clover,
Hundreds of butterflies on the lawn,
 But only one mother the wide
 world over.

George Cooper

Tea Party

My, it's nice
To visit with you!
So glad you could bring
Your little boy, too.

We haven't had
A tea party this way
For ages and ages —
Why, since yesterday!

Mary R. Hurley

Growing Up

My birthday is coming tomorrow,
And then I'm going to be four;
And I'm getting so big that already,
I can open the kitchen door;
I'm very much taller than Baby,
Though today I am only three;
And I'm bigger than Bob-tail the
 puppy,
Who used to be bigger than me.

A boy has two jobs.
One is just being a boy.
The other is growing up to be a man.

Herbert Hoover

Gentle Jesus meek and mild
Look upon a little child
Make me loving, as Thou art
Come and dwell within my heart.
                              Amen.

Mrs. William H. Dietz

Help us to do the things we should
To be to others kind and good
In all our work in all our play
To grow more loving every day.
                              Amen.

Mrs. William H. Dietz

Don't Give Up

If you've tried and have not won,
  Never stop for crying;
All that's great and good is done
  Just by patient trying.

If by easy work you beat,
  Who the more will prize you?
Gaining victory from defeat,
  That's the test that tries you.

Phoebe Cary

The Children's Hour

Between the dark and the daylight,
  When the night is beginning to
    lower,
Comes a pause in the day's
    occupations,
  That is known as the Children's
    Hour.

I hear in the chamber above me
  The patter of little feet,
The sound of a door that is opened,
  And voices soft and sweet.

From my study I see in the
    lamplight,
  Descending the broad hall stair,
Grave Alice, and laughing Allegra,
  And Edith with golden hair.

A whisper, and then a silence:
  Yet I know by their merry eyes
They are plotting and planning
    together
  To take me by surprise.

A sudden rush from the stairway,
  A sudden raid from the hall!
By three doors left unguarded,
  They enter my castle wall!

They climb up into my turret
  O'er the arms and back of my
    chair;
If I try to escape, they surround me;
  They seem to be everywhere.

They almost devour me with kisses,
  Their arms about me entwine,
Till I think of the Bishop of Bingen
  In his Mouse-Tower on the Rhine!

Do you think, O blue-eyed banditti,
  Because you have scaled the wall,
Such an old moustache as I am
  Is not a match for you all?

I have you fast in my fortress,
  And will not let you depart,
But put you down into the dungeon
  In the round-tower of my heart.

And there will I keep you forever,
  Yes, forever and a day,
Till the walls shall crumble to ruin,
  And moulder in dust away!

Henry Wadsworth Longfellow

Even a child is known by his doings,
whether his work be pure, and
whether it be right.

The Bible, Proverbs 20:11

Honour thy father and thy mother:
that thy days may be long upon the
land which the Lord thy God giveth
thee.

The Bible, Exodus 20:12

Happy Memories

On the merry, merry, merry-go-
    round,
The horses go up and the horses go
    down.
Faster and faster they paw and
    prance
In a happy-go-lucky, jerky dance.

On the merry, merry, merry-go-
    round
There's never time for a sigh or
    frown.
In all the world there's no more fun.
I ought to know, I rode on one!

(On the Merry, Merry-Go-Round)
        Dorothy McGrath Martin

Merry-Go-Round

Purple horses with orange manes,
  Elephants pink and blue,
Tigers and lions that never were
    seen
  In circus parade or zoo!
Bring out your money and choose
    your steed,
  And prance to delightsome
    sound.
What fun if the world would turn
    some day
  Into a Merry-Go-Round.

Rachel Field

Song for a Little House

I'm glad our house is a little house,
  Not too tall nor too wide;
I'm glad the hovering butterflies
  Feel free to come inside.

Our little house is a friendly house,
  It is not shy or vain;
It gossips with the talking trees,
  And makes friends with the rain.

And quick leaves cast a shimmer of
    green
  Against our whited walls,
And in the phlox the courteous bees
  Are paying duty calls.

Christopher Morley

Slumber Party

My sister had a slumber party.
Girls giggled and ate till almost
    dawn.
They did not sleep nor did they
    slumber.
So why call it a slumber party?
When they just giggled and ate the
    whole night long.

Carson McCullers

The Hut

We built a hut, my brother and I,
Over a sandy pit,
With twigs that bowed and met
    above
And leaves to cover it.

And there we sat when all around
The rain came pouring down.
We knew if we were out in it
We'd both be sure to drown.

And though in puddles at our feet
Drops gathered from the sky,
We smiled through strands of
    dripping hair,
Because we felt so dry.

Hilda Van Stockum

The Swing

How do you like to go up in a swing,
  Up in the air so blue?
Oh, I do think it the pleasantest
    thing
  Ever a child can do!

Up in the air and over the wall,
  Till I can see so wide,
Rivers and trees and cattle and all
  Over the countryside —

Till I look down on the garden green
  Down on the roof so brown —
Up in the air I go flying again,
  Up in the air and down!

Robert Louis Stevenson

The Postman

Eight o'clock,
The postman's knock!
Five letters for Papa;
  One for Lou,
  And none for you,
And three for dear Mamma.

Christina Rossetti

Daffodils

I wandered lonely as a cloud
  That floats on high o'er vales and
    hills,
When all at once I saw a crowd,
  A host, of golden daffodils;
Beside the lake, beneath the trees,
Fluttering and dancing in the
    breeze.

Continuous as the stars that shine
  And twinkle on the Milky Way,
They stretched in never-ending line
  Along the margin of a bay:
Ten thousand saw I at a glance,
Tossing their heads in sprightly
    dance.

The waves beside them danced, but
    they
  Out-did the sparkling waves in
    glee:
A poet could not but be gay,
  In such a jocund company:
I gazed — and gazed — but little
    thought
What wealth the show to me had
    brought:

For oft, when on my couch I lie
  In vacant or in pensive mood,
They flash upon that inward eye
  Which is the bliss of solitude;
And then my heart with pleasure
    fills,
And dances with the daffodils.

William Wordsworth

117

Break, Break, Break

Break, break, break,
　On thy cold gray stones, O Sea!
And I would that my tongue could
　　utter
The thoughts that arise in me.

O well for the fisherman's boy,
　That he shouts with his sister at
　　play!
O well for the sailor lad,
　That he sings in his boat on the
　　bay!

And the stately ships go on
　To their haven under the hill;
But O for the touch of a vanish'd
　hand,
　And the sound of a voice that is
　　still.

Break, break, break,
　At the foot of thy crags, O Sea!
But the tender grace of a day that is
　dead
Will never come back to me.

Alfred Tennyson

I Love to Tell the Story

I love to tell the story
Of unseen things above,
Of Jesus and His glory,
Of Jesus and His love.
I love to tell the story,
Because I know 'tis true;
It satisfies my longings
As nothing else could do.

I love to tell the story;
More wonderful it seems
Than all the golden fancies
Of all our golden dreams.
I love to tell the story,
It did so much for me;
And that is just the reason
I tell it now to thee.

I love to tell the story;
'Tis pleasant to repeat

What seems, each time I tell it,
More wonderfully sweet.
I love to tell the story,
For some have never heard
The message of salvation
From God's own holy Word.

I love to tell the story;
For those who know it best
Seem hungering and thirsting
To hear it, like the rest.
And when, in scenes of glory,
I sing the new, new song,
'Twill be the old, old story,
That I have loved so long.

I love to tell the story,
'Twill be my theme in glory
To tell the old, old story
Of Jesus and His love.

Katherine Hankey

Little Girl's Heart

A little girl's heart must be wide and
　deep,
To hold all the things that she likes to
　keep;
A curly-haired doll that holds out its
　hands
And walks and talks when occasion
　demands.

A bright colored bow, her favorite
　book,
A little toy stove that really will cook;
A gay, cheery song, to sing when
　she's glad,
A corner to hide in (when she is
　bad).

There is plenty of room for the girl
　next door
And the blue silk dress in the
　downtown store;
A soft fluffy kitten with playful
　charms
And a welcome spot in her mother's
　arms.

Reginald Holmes

When I Was One-and-Twenty

When I was one-and-twenty
  I heard a wise man say,
"Give crowns and pounds and
      guineas
  But not your heart away;
Give pearls away and rubies
  But keep your fancy free."
But I was one-and-twenty,
  No use to talk to me.

When I was one-and-twenty
  I heard him say again,
"The heart out of the bosom
  Was never given in vain;
'Tis paid with sighs a-plenty
  And sold for endless rue."
And I am two-and-twenty,
  And oh, 'tis true, 'tis true.

A. E. Housman

The Secret

We have a secret, just we three,
The robin, and I, and the sweet
  cherry-tree;
The bird told the tree, and the tree
  told me,
And nobody knows it but just us
  three.

But of course the robin knows it
  best,
Because he built the — I shan't tell
  the rest;
And laid the four little — something
  in it —
I'm afraid I shall tell it every minute.

But if the tree and the robin don't
  peep,
I'll try my best the secret to keep;
Though I know when the little birds
  fly about
Then the whole secret will be out.

The Popcorn-Popper

The popcorn man
At the park
Has a popping machine
Inside his cart.
  He puts in dry, yellow brown,
  Hard bits of corn
  And soon —
  Afaff afaff afaff —
  The corn begins to laugh
  And dance
  And hop
  And pop, and pop, and pop.

And then —
  I stand
  And hold
  The bag in my hand,
  And the man
  Pours it full
  Of puffy, fluffy, flaky,
  Soft white
    Popcorn.

Dorothy Baruch

119

Sandlot Days

Summer days were sandlot days
  When I was a boy of ten;
High pop flies and R.B.I.'s
  Were all I cared for then.

The field was just a vacant lot
  Just right for playing ball
Where my Louisville Slugger and I
    went down
  On many a strike-three call.

First and second base were seats
  From two old kitchen chairs,
Third and Home — deflated tires
  Too worn to use for spares.

And, oh, how I remember
  That nothing could replace
The thrill of sliding into Home
  Or getting to steal a base.

Strange, but after all these years
  Every now and then
I long for the good old sandlot days
  That came with being ten.

M. P. Flynn

God's Gifts to Me

Birds and bees, flowers and trees,
  sun and moon to see;
Rain and snow, and winds that
  blow, are God's gifts to me.

Night and day, friends for play, all
  my family;
Love and care, and clothes to wear,
  are God's gifts to me.

Thelma Walton

Memory

My mind lets go a thousand things,
Like dates of wars and deaths of
  kings,
And yet recalls the very hour —
'Twas noon by yonder village tower,
And on the last blue noon in May
The wind came briskly up this way,
Crisping the brook beside the road;
Then, pausing here, set down its
  load
Of pine-scents, and shook listlessly
Two petals from that wild-rose tree.

Thomas Aldrich

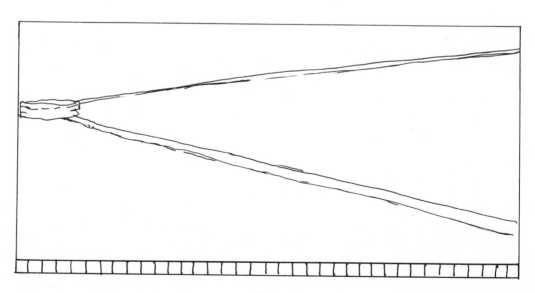

Land of Make Believe

The Owl and the Pussy-Cat went to
sea
In a beautiful pea-green boat,
They took some honey, and plenty of
money
Wrapped up in a five-pound note.
The Owl looked up to the stars
above,
And sang to a small guitar,
"O lovely Pussy, O Pussy, my love,
What a beautiful Pussy you are,
You are,
You are!
What a beautiful Pussy you are!"

Pussy said to the Owl, "You elegant
fowl,
How charmingly sweet you sing!
Oh! let us be married, too long we
have tarried:
But what shall we do for a ring?"

They sailed away, for a year and a
    day,
  To the land where the Bong-tree
    grows;
And there in a wood a Piggy-wig
    stood,
  With a ring at the end of his nose,
        His nose,
        His nose,
  With a ring at the end of his nose.

"Dear Pig, are you willing to sell for
    one shilling
  Your ring?" Said the Piggy, "I
    will."
So they took it away, and were
    married next day
  By the Turkey who lives on the
    hill.
They dined on mince and slices of
    quince,
  Which they ate with a runcible
    spoon;
And hand in hand, on the edge of
    the sand,
  They danced by the light of the
    moon,
        The moon,
        The moon,
  They danced by the light of the
    moon.

                (The Owl and the Pussy-Cat)
                        Edward Lear

The Doze

Through dangly woods the aimless
    Doze
A-dripping and a-dribbling goes.
His company no beast enjoys.
He makes a sort of hopeless noise
Between a snuffle and a snort.
His hair is neither long nor short;
His tail gets caught on briars and
    bushes,
As through the undergrowth he
    pushes.
His ears are big, but not much use.
He lives on blackberries and juice
And anything that he can get.

His feet are clumsy, wide and wet,
Slip-slopping through the bog and
    heather
All in the wild and weepy weather.
His young are many and maltreat
    him;
But only hungry creatures eat him.
He jokes about his mossy holes,
Disturbing sleepless mice and
    moles,
And what he wants he never
    knows —
The damp, despised, and aimless
    Doze.

James Reeves

Twinkle, Twinkle, Little Bat

Twinkle, twinkle, little bat!
How I wonder what you're at?
Up above the world you fly,
Like a tea-tray in the sky.

Lewis Carroll

Jabberwocky

'Twas brillig, and the slithy toves
  Did gyre and gimble in the wabe:
All mimsy were the borogoves,
  And the mome raths outgrabe.

"Beware the Jabberwock, my son!
  The jaws that bite, the claws that
    catch!
Beware the Jubjub bird, and shun
  The frumious Bandersnatch!"

He took his vorpal sword in hand:
  Long time the manxome foe he
    sought —
So rested he by the Tumtum tree,
  And stood awhile in thought.

And, as in uffish thought he stood,
  The Jabberwock, with eyes
      of flame,
Came whiffling through the tulgey
      wood,
  And burbled as it came!

One, two! One, two! And through
    and through
  The vorpal blade went snicker-
      snack!
He left it dead, and with its head
  He went galumphing back.

"And hast thou slain the
    Jabberwock?
  Come to my arms, my beamish
      boy!
O frabjous day! Callooh! Callay!"
  He chortled in his joy.

'Twas brillig, and the slithy toves
  Did gyre and gimble in the wabe:
All mimsy were the borogoves,
  And the mome raths outgrabe.

Lewis Carroll

The Land of Story-Books

At evening when the lamp is lit,
Around the fire my parents sit;
They sit at home and talk and sing,
And do not play at anything.

Now, with my little gun, I crawl
All in the dark along the wall,
And follow round the forest track
Away behind the sofa back.

There, in the night, where none can
      spy,
All in my hunter's camp I lie,
And play at books that I have read
Till it is time to go to bed.

These are the hills, these are the
      woods,
There are my starry solitudes;
And there the river by whose brink
The roaring lions come to drink.

I see the others far away
As if in firelit camp they lay,
And I, like to an Indian scout,
Around their party prowled about.

So, when my nurse comes in for me,
Home I return across the sea,
And go to bed with backward looks
At my dear Land of Story-books.

Robert Louis Stevenson

The Duel

The gingham dog and the calico cat
Side by side on the table sat;
'Twas half-past twelve, and (what do
    you think!)
Nor one nor t'other had slept a wink!
    The old Dutch clock and the
        Chinese plate
    Appeared to know as sure as fate
There was going to be a terrible spat.
    (*I wasn't there; I simply state*
    What was told to me by the Chinese
        plate!)

The gingham dog went, "bow-
    wow-wow!"
And the calico cat replied, "mee-
    ow!"
The air was littered, an hour or so,
With bits of gingham and calico,
    While the old Dutch clock in the
        chimneyplace
    Up with its hands before its face,
For it always dreaded a family row!
    (*Now mind: I'm only telling you*
    What the old Dutch clock declares is
        true!)

The Chinese plate looked very blue,
And wailed, "Oh, dear! what shall
    we do!"
But the gingham dog and the calico
    cat
Wallowed this way and tumbled
    that,
    Employing every tooth and claw
    In the awfullest way you ever
        saw —
And, oh! how the gingham and
    calico flew!
    (*Don't fancy I exaggerate —*
    I got my news from the Chinese
        plate!)

Next morning, where the two had
    sat
They found no trace of dog or cat;
And some folks think unto this day
That burglars stole that pair away!
    But the truth about the cat and pup
    Is this: they ate each other up!
Now what do you really think of
    that!
    (*The Old Dutch clock it told me so,*
    And that is how I came to know.)

Eugene Field

The Jumblies

They went to sea in a sieve, they did;
    In a sieve they went to sea:
In spite of all their friends could say,
On a winter's morn, on a stormy
    day,
    In a sieve they went to sea.
And when the sieve turned round
    and round,
And everyone cried, "You'll all be
    drowned!"
They called aloud, "Our sieve ain't
    big;
But we don't care a button, we don't
    care a fig:
    In a sieve we'll go to sea!"
    Far and few, far and few,
    Are the lands where the
        Jumblies live:
    Their heads are green, and
        their hands are blue;
    And they went to sea in a
        sieve.

Edward Lear

126

A Swing Song

Swing, swing,
Sing, sing,
Here! my throne
and I am a king!
Swing, sing,
Swing, sing,
Farewell, earth,
for I'm on the wing!
Low, high,
Here I fly,
Like a bird
through sunny sky;
Free, free,
Over the lea,
Over the mountain,
over the sea!

Up, down,
Up, down,
Which is the way
to London Town?
Where? Where?
Up in the air,
Close your eyes and
now you are there!
No, no,
Low, low,
Sweeping daisies
with my toe.
Slow, slow,
To and fro,
Slow — slow — slow — slow.

William Allingham

When Mother Reads Aloud

When Mother reads aloud, the past
Seems real as every day;
I hear the tramp of armies vast,
I see the spears and lances cast,
I join the thrilling fray.
Brave knights and ladies fair and
proud
I meet when Mother reads aloud.

When Mother reads aloud, far lands
Seem very near and true;
I cross the desert's gleaming sands,
Or hunt the jungle's prowling
bands,
Or sail the ocean blue.
Far heights, whose peaks the cold
mists shroud,
I scale, when Mother reads aloud.

When Mother reads aloud, I long
For noble deeds to do —
To help the right, redress the wrong;
It seems so easy to be strong,
So simple to be true.
Oh, thick and fast the visions crowd
My eyes, when Mother reads aloud.

Only My Opinion

Is a caterpillar ticklish?
Well, it's always my belief
That he giggles, as he wiggles
Across a hairy leaf.

Monica Shannon

The Little Man Who Wasn't There

As I was going up the stair
I met a man who wasn't there!
He wasn't there again today!
I wish, I *wish* he'd stay away!

Hughes Mearns

The Ichthyosaurus

There once was an Ichthyosaurus
Who lived when the earth was all
porous,
But he fainted with shame
When he first heard his name,
And departed a long time before us.

127

There Once Was a Puffin

Oh, there once was a Puffin
Just the shape of a muffin,
And he lived on an island
In the
      bright
          blue
              sea!

He ate little fishes,
That were most delicious,
And he had them for supper
And he
      had
          them
              for tea.

But this poor little Puffin
He couldn't play nothin',
For he hadn't anybody
To
   play
      with
         at all.

So he sat on his island,
And he cried for awhile, and
He felt very lonely
And he
      felt
         very
            small.

Then along came the fishes,
And they said, "If you wishes,
You can have us for playmates,
Instead
      of
        for
          tea!"

So now they play together,
In all sorts of weather,
And the Puffin eats pancakes,
Like you
      and
        like
          me.

Florence Page Jaques

The Invisible Playmate

When the other children go,
  Though there's no one seems to
    see
And there's no one seems to know,
  Fanny comes and plays with me.

She has yellow curly hair
  And her dress is always blue,
And she always plays quite fair
  Everything I tell her to.

People say she isn't there —
  They step over her at play
And they sit down in her chair
  In the very rudest way.

It is queer they cannot know
  When she's there for me to see!
When the other children go
  Fanny comes and plays with me.

Margaret Widdemer

The Land of Counterpane

When I was sick and lay a-bed,
I had two pillows at my head,
And all my toys beside me lay
To keep me happy all the day.

And sometimes for an hour or so
I watched my leaden soldiers go,
With different uniforms and drills,
Among the bed-clothes, through the
    hills;

And sometimes sent my ships in
    fleets
All up and down among the sheets;
Or brought my trees and houses out,
And planted cities all about.

I was the giant great and still
That sits upon the pillow-hill,
And sees before him, dale and plain,
The pleasant land of counterpane.

Robert Louis Stevenson

Escape at Bedtime

The lights from the parlour and
    kitchen shone out
  Through the blinds and the
    windows and bars;
And high overhead and all moving
    about,
  There were thousands of millions
    of stars.

There ne'er were such thousands of
    leaves on a tree,
  Nor of people in church or the
    Park,
As the crowds of the stars that
    looked down upon me,
  And that glittered and winked in
    the dark.

The Dog, and the Plough, and the
    Hunter, and all,
  And the Star of the Sailor, and
    Mars,
These shone in the sky, and the pail
    by the wall
  Would be half full of water and
    stars.

They saw me at last, and they chased
    me with cries,
  And they soon had me packed into
    bed;
But the glory kept shining bright in
    my eyes,
  And the stars going round in my
    head.

Robert Louis Stevenson

Wish

If I could wish
I'd be a fish
(For just a day or two)
To flip and flash
And dart and splash
With nothing else to do,
And never anyone to say,
"Are you quite sure you washed
    today?"
I'd like it, wouldn't you?

Dorothy Brown Thompson

My Rocking Chair

I have a little rocking chair
That hides a tiny squeak
    somewhere;
It's quite as if some baby Elf
Were singing to his little self.
I rock and rock, so I can see
Just what he tries to say to me.
My Mother says, "Good gracious,
    child!
That noise will surely drive me
    wild!"
But that's because she doesn't know
An Elf is singing down below!

Doris I. Bateman

Daisies

At evening when I go to bed
I see the stars shine overhead.
They are the little daisies white
That dot the meadow of the night.

And often while I'm dreaming so,
Across the sky the moon will go.
It is a lady, sweet and fair,
Who comes to gather daisies there.

For, when at morning I arise,
There's not a star left in the skies.
She's picked them all
And dropped them down
Into the meadows of the town.

Frank Dempster Sherman

Block City

What are you able to build with your
    blocks?
Castles and palaces, temples and
    docks.
Rain may keep raining, and others
    go roam,
But I can be happy and building at
    home.

Let the sofa be mountains, the carpet
    be sea,
There I'll establish a city for me:
A kirk and a mill and a palace beside,
And a harbor as well where my
    vessels may ride.

Great is the palace with pillar and
    wall,
A sort of a tower on the top of it all,
And steps coming down in an
    orderly way
To where my toy vessels lie safe in
    the bay.

This one is sailing and that one is
    moored:
Hark to the song of the sailors on
    board!
And see on the steps of my palace,
    the kings
Coming and going with presents
    and things!

Now I have done with it, down let it
    go!
All in a moment the town is laid low.
Block upon block lying scattered and
    free,
What is there left of my town by the
    sea?

Yet as I saw it, I see it again,
The kirk and the palace, the ships
    and the men,
And as long as I live and where'er I
    may be,
I'll always remember my town by the
    sea.

Robert Louis Stevenson

Mouths

I wish I had two little mouths
Like my two hands and feet —
A little mouth to talk with
And one that just could eat.

Because it seems to me mouths have
So many things to do —
All the time they want to talk
They are supposed to chew!

Dorothy Aldis

The Sugar-Plum Tree

Have you ever heard of the Sugar-
    Plum Tree?
  'Tis a marvel of great renown!
It blooms on the shore of the
    Lollipop Sea
  In the garden of Shut-Eye Town.

Eugene Field

Lessons to Learn

A little kingdom I possess
    Where thoughts and feelings
        dwell;
And very hard the task I find
    Of governing it well.

I do not ask for any crown
    But that which all may win;
Nor try to conquer any world
    Except the one within.

(My Kingdom)
Louisa May Alcott

Recessional

God of our fathers, known of old,
  Lord of our far-flung battle-line,
Beneath whose awful Hand we hold
  Dominion over palm and pine—
Lord God of Hosts, be with us yet,
Lest we forget — lest we forget!

The tumult and the shouting dies;
  The Captains and the Kings
    depart:
Still stands thine ancient sacrifice,
  An humble and a contrite heart.
Lord God of Hosts, be with us yet,
Lest we forget — lest we forget!

Far-called, our navies melt away;
  On dune and headland sinks the
    fire:
Lo, all our pomp of yesterday
  Is one with Nineveh and Tyre!
Judge of the Nations, spare us yet,
Lest we forget — lest we forget!

If, drunk with sight of power, we
    loose
  Wild tongues that have not thee in
    awe,
Such boastings as the Gentiles use,
  Or lesser breeds without the
    Law —
Lord God of Hosts, be with us yet,
Lest we forget — lest we forget!

For heathen heart that puts her trust
  In reeking tube and iron shard,
All valiant dust that builds on dust,
  And, guarding, calls not thee to
    guard,
For frantic boast and foolish word —
Thy mercy on thy People, Lord!

Rudyard Kipling

Every Day

Love the beautiful,
  Seek out the true,
Wish for the good,
  And the best do!

Felix Mendelssohn

Success

Success is speaking words of praise,
In cheering other people's ways,
In doing just the best you can,
With every task and every plan.

It's silence when your speech would
    hurt,
Politeness when your neighbor's
    curt.
It's deafness when the scandal flows,
And sympathy with others' woes.

It's loyalty when duty calls,
It's courage when disaster falls,
It's patience when the hours are
    long,
It's found in laughter and in song.

It's in the silent time of prayer.
In happiness and in despair,
In all of life and nothing less,
We find the thing we call success.

No bees, no honey;
No work, no money.

Be True

Thou must be true thyself
  If thou the truth wouldst teach;
Thy soul must overflow if thou
  Another's soul wouldst reach!
It needs the overflow of heart
  To give the lips full speech.

Think truly, and thy thoughts
  Shall the world's famine feed;
Speak truly, and each word of thine
  Shall be a fruitful seed;
Live truly, and thy life shall be
  A great and noble creed.

Horatius Bonar

Four Things

Four things a man must learn to do
If he would make his record true:
To think without confusion clearly;
To love his fellow-men sincerely;
To act from honest motives purely;
To trust in God and Heaven
    securely.

Henry Van Dyke

Lend a Hand

I am only one,
But still I am one.
I cannot do everything,
But still I can do something;
And because I cannot do everything
I will not refuse to do the something
    that I can do.

Edward Everett Hale

We always have time enough, if we use it aright.

Johann Wolfgang Von Goethe

The Oak

Live thy life,
    Young and old,
Like yon oak,
Bright in spring
    Living gold;

Summer-rich
    Then; and then
Autumn-changed,
Soberer-hued
    Gold again.

All his leaves
    Fallen at length,
Look, he stands,
Trunk and bough,
    Naked strength.

Alfred Tennyson

When Jesus Walked Upon the Earth

When Jesus walked upon the earth
    He didn't talk with kings,
He talked with simple people
    Of doing friendly things.

He didn't praise the conquerors
    And all their hero host;
He said the very greatest
    Were those who loved the most.

He didn't speak of mighty deeds
    And victories. He spoke
Of feeding hungry people
    And cheering lonely folk.

I'm glad His words were simple words
    Just meant for me and you,
The things He asked were simple things
    That even I can do.

Marion Brown Shelton

135

Be Like the Bird

Be like the bird, who
Halting in his flight
On limb too slight
Feels it give way beneath him,
Yet sings
Knowing he hath wings.

Victor Hugo

Footprints made on the sands of time were never made sitting down.

A winner never quits;
A quitter never wins.

A penny saved is a penny earned.

Practice makes perfect.

Lost

Lost, yesterday, somewhere
between sunrise and sunset,
two golden hours,
each set with sixty
diamond minutes.
No reward is offered
for they are gone forever.

Doubts

Our doubts are traitors,
And make us lose the good we oft
    might win,
By fearing to attempt.

William Shakespeare

To-day

Build a little fence of trust
    Around to-day;
Fill the space with loving deeds
    And therein stay.
Look not through the sheltering bars
    Upon to-morrow;
God will help thee bear what comes
    Of joy or sorrow.

Mary Frances Butts

He that is slow to anger is better than
    the mighty;
And he that ruleth his spirit than he
    that taketh a city.

The Bible, Proverbs 16:32

A soft answer turneth away wrath:
But grievous words stir up anger.

The Bible, Proverbs 15:1

A talebearer revealeth secrets:
But he that is of a faithful spirit con-
    cealeth the matter.

The Bible, Proverbs 11:13

A good name is rather to be chosen
    than great riches,
And loving favour rather than silver
    and gold.

The Bible, Proverbs 22:1

But they that wait upon the Lord
    shall renew their strength;
They shall mount up with wings as
    eagles;
They shall run, and not be weary;
And they shall walk, and not faint.

The Bible, Isaiah 40:31

How happy are those who know
    their need for God,
  for the kingdom of Heaven
    is theirs!
How happy are those who know
    what sorrow means,
  for they will be given courage and
    comfort!
Happy are those who claim nothing,
  for the whole earth will belong to
    them!
Happy are those who are hungry
    and thirsty for true goodness,
  for they will be fully satisfied!
Happy are the merciful,
  for they will have mercy shown to
    them!
Happy are the utterly sincere,
  for they will see God!
Happy are those who make peace,
  for they will be known as sons of
    God!
Happy are those who have suffered
    persecution for the cause of
    goodness,
  for the kingdom of Heaven is
    theirs!
And what happiness will be yours
    when people blame you
  and ill-treat you and say all kinds
    of slanderous things against
    you for my sake!

The Bible, Matthew 5:3-12, Phillips

Blessed is the man
  that walketh not in the
    counsel of the ungodly,
  nor standeth in the way of sinners,
  nor sitteth in the seat of the
    scornful.
But his delight
  is in the law of the Lord;
  and in his law doth he meditate
    day and night.
And he shall be like a tree
  planted by the rivers of water,
  that bringeth forth his fruit in his
    season;
  his leaf also shall not wither;
  and whatsoever he doeth shall
    prosper.

The Bible, Psalm 1:1-3

Go to the Ant

Go to the ant, thou sluggard;
Consider her ways, and be wise:
Which having no guide,
Overseer, or ruler,
Provideth her meat in the summer,
And gathereth her food in the
    harvest.

The Bible, Proverbs 6:6-8

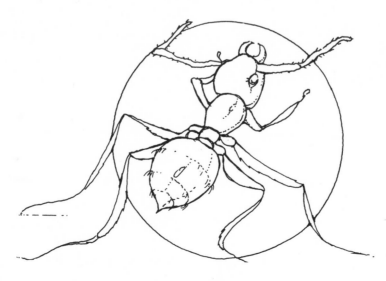

Love and Gratitude

He prayeth best, who loveth best
All things both great and small;
For the dear God who loveth us,
He made and loveth all.

Samuel Taylor Coleridge
(from The Rime of the
Ancient Mariner)

Two little eyes to look to God,
Two little ears to hear His word,
Two little feet to walk His ways,
Hands to serve Him all my days.

One little tongue to speak His truth,
One little heart for Him in youth,
Take them, O Jesus, let them be
Always willing, true to Thee.

(Two Little Eyes)

A Child's Offering

The wise may bring their learning,
  The rich may bring their wealth,
And some may bring their
    greatness,
  And some bring strength and
    health;
We, too, would bring our treasures
  To offer to the King;
We have no wealth or learning:
  What shall we children bring?

We'll bring Him hearts that love
    Him;
  We'll bring Him thankful praise,
And young souls meekly striving
  To walk in holy ways:
And these shall be the treasures
  We offer to the King,
And these are gifts that even
  The poorest child may bring.

We'll bring the little duties
  We have to do each day;
We'll try our best to please Him,
  At home, at school, at play:
And better are these treasures
  To offer to our King,
Than richest gifts without them;
  Yet these a child may bring.

The Book of Praise for Children

They that go down to the sea in
    ships,
  that do business in great waters;
These see the works of the Lord, and
  his wonders in the deep.
For he commandeth, and raiseth the
    stormy wind,
  which lifteth up the waves
    thereof.
They mount up to the heaven, they
  go down again to the depths:
  Their soul is melted because of
    trouble.

They reel to and fro, and stagger
    like a drunken man,
  And are at their wits' end.
Then they cry unto the Lord in their
    trouble,
  and he bringeth them out of
    their distresses.
He maketh the storm a calm, so that
  the waves thereof are still.
Then are they glad because they be
    quiet;
  so he bringeth them unto their
    desired haven.
Oh that men would praise the Lord
    for his goodness,
  and for his wonderful works to the
    children of men!

The Bible, Psalm 107:23-31

Praise ye the Lord.
Praise God in his sanctuary:
Praise him in the firmament of
    his power.
Praise him for his mighty acts:
Praise him according to his
    excellent greatness.
Praise him with the sound of the
    trumpet:
Praise him with the psaltery and
    harp.
Praise him with the timbrel and
    dance:
Praise him with stringed
    instruments and organs.
Praise him upon the loud cymbals:
Praise him upon the high sounding
    cymbals.
Let every thing that hath breath
    praise the Lord.
Praise ye the Lord.

The Bible, Psalm 150

Woodman, Spare That Tree

Woodman, spare that tree!
  Touch not a single bough!
In youth it sheltered me,
  And I'll protect it now.
'Twas my forefather's hand
  That placed it near his cot;
There, woodman, let it stand,
  Thy axe shall harm it not!

That old familiar tree,
  Whose glory and renown
Are spread o'er land and sea,
  And wouldst thou hew it down?
Woodman, forbear thy stroke!
  Cut not its earth-bound ties;
O, spare that aged oak,
  Now towering to the skies!

When but an idle boy
  I sought its grateful shade;
In all their gushing joy
  Here too my sisters played.
My mother kissed me here;
  My father pressed my hand —
Forgive this foolish tear,
  But let that old oak stand!

My heart-strings round thee cling,
  Close as thy bark, old friend!
Here shall the wild-bird sing,
  And still thy branches bend.
Old tree! the storm still brave!
  And, woodman, leave the spot;
While I've a hand to save,
  Thy axe shall harm it not.

George Pope Morris

Deeds of Kindness

Suppose the little Cowslip
  Should hang its golden cup
And say, "I'm such a little flower
  I'd better not grow up!"
How many a weary traveller
  Would miss its fragrant smell,
How many a little child would grieve
  To lose it from the dell!

Suppose the glistening Dewdrop
  Upon the grass should say,
"What can a little dewdrop do?
  I'd better roll away!"
The blade on which it rested,
  Before the day was done,
Without a drop to moisten it,
  Would wither in the sun.

Suppose the little Breezes,
  Upon a summer's day,
Should think themselves too small to
    cool
  The traveller on his way:
Who would not miss the smallest
  And softest ones that blow,
And think they made a great mistake
  If they were acting so?

How many deeds of kindness
  A little child can do,
Although it has but little strength
  And little wisdom too!
It wants a loving spirit
  Much more than strength,
    to prove
How many things a child may do
  For others by its love.

The Night Has a Thousand Eyes

The night has a thousand eyes,
  And the day but one;
Yet the light of the bright world dies
  With the dying sun.

The mind has a thousand eyes,
  And the heart but one;
Yet the light of a whole life dies
  When love is done.

Francis William Bourdillon

Bless the Lord, O my soul:
And all that is within me, bless
  his holy name.
Bless the Lord, O my soul,
And forget not all his benefits:
Who forgiveth all thine iniquities;
Who healeth all thy diseases;
Who redeemeth thy life from
  destruction;
Who crowneth thee with loving-
  kindness and tender mercies;
Who satisfieth thy mouth with good
  things;
So that thy youth is renewed like the
  eagle's.

The Bible, Psalm 103:1-5

What Can I Give Him?

What can I give Him,
  Poor as I am?
If I were a shepherd,
  I would bring a lamb;
If I were a wise man
  I would do my part, —
Yet what can I give Him,
  Give Him my heart.

Christina Rossetti

Thanksgiving Hymn

We gather together to ask the Lord's
blessing;
He chastens and hastens his will
to make known;
The wicked oppressing now cease
from distressing:
Sing praises to his Name; he
forgets not his own.

Beside us to guide us, our God with
us joining,
Ordaining, maintaining his
Kingdom divine;
So from the beginning the fight we
were winning;
Thou, Lord, wast at our side: all
glory be thine.

We all do extol thee, thou Leader
triumphant,
And pray that thou still our
Defender wilt be.
Let thy congregation escape
tribulation:
Thy Name be ever prais'd! O
Lord, make us free!

Words translated by Theodore Baker

Beshrew me but I love her heartily;
For she is wise, if I can judge of her,
And fair she is, if that mine eyes be
true,
And true she is as she hath proved
herself,
And therefore, like herself, wise, fair
and true,
Shall she be placed in my constant
soul.

*William Shakespeare
(from The Merchant of Venice)*

My Country and Its Heroes

Listen, my children, and you shall
    hear
Of the midnight ride of Paul Revere,
On the eighteenth of April, in
    seventy-five;
Hardly a man is now alive
Who remembers that famous day
    and year.
He said to his friend, "If the British
    march
By land or sea from the town tonight,
Hang a lantern aloft in the belfry
    arch
Of the North Church tower as a
    signal light, —
One, if by land, and two, if by sea;
And I on the opposite shore will be,
Ready to ride and spread the alarm
Through every Middlesex village
    and farm,
For the country folk to be up and to
    arm."

Then he said, "Good night!" and
  with muffled oar
Silently rowed to the Charleston
  shore,
Just as the moon rose over the bay,
Where swinging wide at her
  moorings lay
The *Somerset*, British man-of-war;
A phantom ship, with each mast
  and spar
Across the moon like a prison bar,
And a huge black hulk, that was
  magnified
By its own reflection in the tide.

Meanwhile, his friend, through
  alley and street,
Wanders and watches with eager
  ears,
Till in the silence around him he
  hears
The muster of men at the barrack
  door,
The sound of arms, and the tramp of
  feet,
And the measured tread of the
  grenadiers,
Marching down to their boats on the
  shore.

Then he climbed the tower of the
  Old North Church
By the wooden stairs, with stealthy
  tread,
To the belfry-chamber overhead,
And startled the pigeons from their
  perch
On the somber rafters, that round
  him made
Masses and moving shapes of
  shade, —
By the trembling ladder, steep and
  tall,
To the highest window in the wall,
Where he paused to listen and look
  down
A moment on the roofs of the town,
And the moonlight flowing over all.

Beneath in the churchyard, lay the
  dead,
In their night-encampment on the
  hill,

Wrapped in silence so deep and still
That he could hear, like a sentinel's
  tread,
The watchful night-wind, as it went
Creeping along from tent to tent,
And seeming to whisper, "All is
  Well!"
A moment only he feels the spell
Of the place and the hour, and the
  secret dread
Of the lonely belfry and the dead;
For suddenly all his thoughts are
  bent
On a shadowy something far away,
Where the river widens to meet the
  bay, —
A line of black that bends and
  floats
On the rising tide, like a bridge of
  boats.

Meanwhile, impatient to mount and
  ride,
Booted and spurred, with a heavy
  stride
On the opposite shore walked Paul
  Revere.
Now he patted his horse's side,
Now gazed at the landscape far and
  near,
Then, impetuous, stamped the
  earth,
And turned and tightened his
  saddle-girth;
But mostly he watched with eager
  search
The belfry-tower of the Old North
  Church,
As it rose above the graves on the
  hill,
Lonely and spectral and somber and
  still.
And lo! as he looks, on the belfry's
  height
A glimmer, and then a gleam of
  light!
He springs to the saddle, the bridle
  he turns,
But lingers and gazes, till full on his
  sight
A second lamp in the belfry burns!

A hurry of hoofs in a village street,
A shape in the moonlight, a bulk in
the dark,
And beneath, from the pebbles, in
passing, a spark
Struck out by a steed flying fearless
and fleet:
That was all! And yet, through the
gloom and the light,
The fate of a nation was riding that
night;
And the spark struck out by that
steed, in his flight
Kindled the land into flame with its
heat.
He has left the village and mounted
the steep,
And beneath him, tranquil and
broad and deep,
Is the Mystic, meeting the ocean
tides;
And under the alders that skirt its
edge,
Now soft on the sand, now loud on
the ledge,
Is heard the tramp of his steed as he
rides.

It was twelve by the village clock,
When he crossed the bridge into
Medford town.
He heard the crowing of the cock,
And the barking of the farmer's dog,
And felt the damp of the river fog,
That rises after the sun goes down.
It was one by the village clock,
When he galloped into Lexington.
He saw the gilded weathercock
Swim in the moonlight as he passed.
And the meeting-house windows,
blank and bare,
Gaze at him with a spectral glare,
As if they already stood aghast
At the bloody work they would look
upon.
It was two by the village clock,
When he came to the bridge in
Concord town.
He heard the bleating of the flock,
And the twitter of birds among the
trees,

And felt the breath of the morning
breeze
Blowing over the meadows brown.
And one was safe and asleep in his
bed
Who at the bridge would be first to
fall,
Who that day would be lying dead,
Pierced by a British musket-ball.

You know the rest. In the books you
have read,
How the British Regulars fired and
fled, —
How the farmers gave them ball for
ball,
From behind each fence and
farmyard wall,
Chasing the red-coats down the
lane,
Then crossing the fields to emerge
again
Under the trees at the turn of the
road,
And only pausing to fire and load.

So through the night rode Paul
Revere;
And so through the night went his
cry of alarm
To every Middlesex village and
farm, —
A cry of defiance and not of fear,
A voice in the darkness, a knock at
the door,
And a word that shall echo
forevermore!
For, borne on the night-wind of the
Past,
Through all our history, to the last,
In the hour of darkness and peril and
need,
The people will waken and listen to
hear
The hurrying hoof-beats of that
steed,
And the midnight message of Paul
Revere.

(Paul Revere's Ride)
Henry Wadsworth Longfellow

The Star-Spangled Banner

O say, can you see, by the dawn's
early light,
What so proudly we hailed at the
twilight's last gleaming,
Whose broad stripes and bright stars,
through the perilous fight,
O'er the ramparts we watched
were so gallantly streaming!
And the rockets' red glare, the
bombs bursting in air,
Gave proof through the night that
our flag was still there.
O say, does that star-spangled
banner yet wave
O'er the land of the free and the
home of the brave?

On the shore, dimly seen through
the mists of the deep,
Where the foe's haughty host in
dread silence reposes,
What is that which the breeze, o'er
the towering steep,
As it fitfully blows, half conceals,
half discloses?
Now it catches the gleam of the
morning's first beam,
In full glory reflected now shines on
the stream.
'Tis the star-spangled banner! O
long may it wave
O'er the land of the free and the
home of the brave!

And where is that band who so
vauntingly swore
That the havoc of war and the
battle's confusion
A home and a country should leave
us no more?
Their blood has washed out their
foul footsteps' pollution.
No refuge could save the hireling
and slave
From the terror of flight, or the
gloom of the grave:
And the star-spangled banner in
triumph doth wave
O'er the land of the free and the
home of the brave!

O thus be it ever when free men shall
stand
Between their loved homes and
the war's desolation!
Blest with victory and peace, may
the heaven-rescued land
Praise the Power that hath made
and preserved us a nation.
Then conquer we must, when our
cause it is just,
And this be our motto: "In God is
our trust!"
And the star-spangled banner in
triumph shall wave
O'er the land of the free and the
home of the brave!

Francis Scott Key

The American Flag

A thoughtful mind, when it sees a Nation's flag, sees not the flag only, but the nation itself; and whatever may be its symbols, its insignia, he reads chiefly in the flag the Government, the principles, the truths, the history which belong to the Nation that sets it forth.

Henry Ward Beecher

Pledge of Allegiance to the Flag

I pledge allegiance
to the flag of the United States of
    America
and to the republic for which it
    stands,
one nation, under God,*
indivisible,
with liberty and justice for all.

Francis Bellamy

*The words "under God" were added when Dwight Eisenhower was president.

You're a Grand Old Flag

You're a grand old flag,
You're a high flying flag;
And forever in peace may you wave;
You're the emblem of
The land I love,
The home of the free and the brave.
Every heart beats true
Under red, white and blue,
Where there's never a boast or brag;
But should auld acquaintance be
    forgot,
Keep your eye on the grand old flag.

George M. Cohan

I Love America

I love America, where truth can be shouted from the housetops, instead of whispered in dismal cellars hidden from the spies and dictators.

I love America, where families can sleep peacefully without fear of secret seizure and torture in some foul prison, or purged in blood for political reasons.

I love America, where men are truly free men; not living in fear of slavery, exile, or involuntary servitude, while their homes are confiscated and loved ones are turned weeping and sorrowing from their doors.

I love America, where there are equal rights for all, and where people are not forced to hate, persecute, or kill because of religion, race, or creed.

I love America where little children are not forced to suffer for want of bread withheld at the whim of some despot carrying out a plan for greater glory.

I love America, where men can think as they please, and where thought is not regulated by decrees, enforced with bullets and bayonets.

I love America, where there is love, laughter, hope, and opportunity, and not hate, sorrow, dejection, and futility.

I love America, despite her present troubles because free men can cure them.

I love America, and I will gladly give my life to preserve the freedom our forefathers created, so that our children and their descendants can forever enjoy blessings we have inherited.

Franklin E. Jordan

Columbus

Behind him lay the gray Azores,
  Behind the Gates of Hercules;
Before him not the ghost of shores;
  Before him only shoreless seas.
The good mate said: "Now must we
    pray,
  For lo! the very stars are gone.
Brave Admiral, speak, what shall I
    say?"
  "Why, say 'Sail on! sail on! and
    on!' "

"My men grow mutinous day by
    day;
  My men grow ghastly wan and
    weak."
The stout mate thought of home; a
    spray
  Of salt wave washed his swarthy
    cheek.
"What shall I say, brave Admiral,
    say,
  If we sight naught but seas at
    dawn?"
"Why, you shall say at break of day,
  'Sail on! sail on! sail on! and on!' "

They sailed and sailed, as winds
    might blow,
  Until at last the blanched mate
    said,
"Why, now not even God would
    know
  Should I and all my men fall dead.
These very winds forget their way,
  For God from these dread seas is
    gone.
Now speak, brave Admiral, speak
    and say" —
  He said: "Sail on! sail on! and on!"

They sailed. They sailed. Then spake
    the mate:
  "This mad sea shows his teeth
    to-night.
He curls his lip, he lies in wait,
  With lifted teeth, as if to bite!
Brave Admiral, say but one good
    word:
  What shall we do when hope is
    gone?"
The words leapt like a leaping
    sword:
  "Sail on! sail on! sail on! and on!"

Then, pale and worn, he kept his
    deck,
  And peered through darkness.
    Ah, that night
Of all dark nights! And then a
    speck —
  A light! a light! a light! a light!
It grew, a starlit flag unfurled!
  It grew to be Time's burst of dawn.
He gained a world; he gave that
    world
  Its grandest lesson: "On! sail on!"

Joaquin Miller

In Fourteen Hundred and Ninety-
    two
Columbus sailed the ocean blue.
In Fourteen Hundred and Ninety-
    three
Columbus sailed the deep blue sea.
In Fourteen Hundred and Ninety-
    four
Columbus sailed the sea once more.

150

The Pilgrim

Who would true valour see,
  Let him come hither!
One here will constant be,
  Come wind, come weather;
There's no discouragement
Shall make him once relent
His flint-avow'd intent
  To be a Pilgrim.

Whoso beset him round
  With dismal stories,
Do but themselves confound;
  His strength the more is.
No lion can him fright;
He'll with a giant fight;
But he will have a right
  To be a Pilgrim.

Nor enemy, nor friend,
  Can daunt his spirit;
He knows he at the end
  Shall Life inherit: —
Then, fancies, fly away;
He'll not fear what men say:
He'll labour, night and day,
  To be a Pilgrim.

John Bunyan

Washington

He played by the river when he was
  young,
He raced with rabbits along the hills,
He fished for minnows, and climbed
  and swung,
And hooted back at the
  whippoorwills.
Strong and slender and tall he
  grew —
And then, one morning, the bugles
  blew.

Over the hills the summons came,
Over the river's shining rim.
He said that the bugles called his
  name,
He knew that his country needed
  him,
And he answered, "Coming!" and
  marched away
For many a night and many a day.

Perhaps when the marches were hot
  and long
He'd think of the river flowing by
Or, camping under the winter sky,
Would hear the whippoorwill's
  far-off song.
Working or playing, in peace or
  strife,
He loved America all his life!

Nancy Byrd Turner

George Washington

Washington, the brave, the wise,
  the good.
Supreme in war, in council, and in
  peace.
Valiant without ambition, discreet
  without fear, confident without
    presumption.
In disaster, calm; in success,
  moderate; in all, himself.
The hero, the patriot, the Christian.
The father of nations, the friend of
  mankind,
Who, when he had won all,
  renounced all, and sought
  in the bosom of his family
    and of nature,
  retirement, and in the hope
    of religion, immortality.

Inscription at Mount Vernon

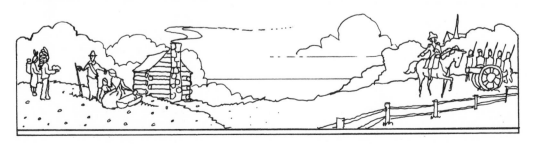

151

Concord Hymn

By the rude bridge that arched the
flood,
   Their flag to April's breeze
      unfurled,
Here once the embattled farmers
stood
   And fired the shot heard round the
      world.

The foe long since in silence slept;
   Alike the conqueror silent sleeps;
And Time the ruined bridge has
swept
   Down the dark stream which
      seaward creeps.

On this green bank, by this soft
stream,
   We set to-day a votive stone;
That memory may their deed
redeem,
   When, like our sires, our sons are
      gone.

Spirit, that made those heroes dare
   To die, and leave their children
      free,
Bid Time and Nature gently spare
   The shaft we raise to them and
      thee.

Ralph Waldo Emerson

Is life so dear, or peace so sweet, as to
be purchased at the price of chains
and slavery? Forbid it, Almighty
God! I know not what course others
may take, but as for me, give me
liberty or give me death.

Patrick Henry

Daniel Boone

Daniel Boone at twenty-one
Came with his tomahawk, knife,
and gun
Home from the French and Indian
War
To North Carolina and the Yadkin
shore.
He married his maid with a golden
band,
Builded his house and cleared his
land;
But the deep woods claimed their
son again
And he turned his face from the
homes of men.
Over the Blue Ridge, dark and lone,
The Mountains of Iron, the Hills of
Stone,
Braving the Shawnee's jealous
wrath,
He made his way on the Warrior's
Path.
Alone he trod the shadowed trails;
But he was lord of a thousand vales
As he roved Kentucky, far and near,
Hunting the buffalo, elk, and deer.
What joy to see, what joy to win
So fair a land for his kith and kin,
Of streams unstained and woods
unhewn!
"Elbow room!" laughed Daniel
Boone.

On the Wilderness Road that his
axmen made
The settlers flocked to the first
stockade;
The deerskin shirts and the coonskin
caps
Filed through the glens and the
mountain gaps;

152

And hearts were high in the fateful
    spring
When the land said, "Nay!" to the
    stubborn king.
While the men of the East of farm
    and town
Strove with the troops of the British
    Crown,
Daniel Boone from a surge of hate
Guarded a nation's westward gate.
Down in the fort in a wave of flame
The Shawnee horde and the Mingo
    came,
And the stout logs shook in a storm
    of lead;
But Boone stood firm and the savage
    fled.
Peace! And the settlers flocked
    anew,
The farm lands spread, the town
    lands grew;
But Daniel Boone was ill at ease
When he saw the smoke in his forest
    trees.
"There'll be no game in the country
    soon.
"Elbow room!" cried Daniel Boone.

Straight as a pine at sixty-five —
Time enough for a man to thrive —
He launched his bateau on Ohio's
    breast
And his heart was glad as he oared it
    west;
There were kindly folk and his own
    true blood
Where great Missouri rolls his flood;
New woods, new streams, and room
    to spare,
And Daniel Boone found comfort
    there.
Yet far he ranged toward the sunset
    still,

Where the Kansas runs and the
    Smoky Hill,
And the prairies toss, by the south
    wind blown:
And he killed his bear on the
    Yellowstone
But ever he dreamed of new
    domains
With vast woods and wilder plains;
Ever he dreamed of a world-to-be
Where there are no bounds and the
    soul is free.
At fourscore-five, still stout and
    hale,
He heard a call to a farther trail;
So he turned his face where the stars
    are strewn;
"Elbow room!" sighed Daniel
    Boone.

Arthur Guiterman

With malice toward none,
With charity for all,
With firmness in the right as God
    gives us to see the right,
Let us strive on to finish the work we
    are in,
To bind up the nation's wounds,
To care for him who shall have borne
    the battle
And for his widow
And his orphan,
To do all which may achieve and
    cherish a just and lasting peace
    among ourselves
And with all nations.

Abraham Lincoln
(from Second Inaugural Address)

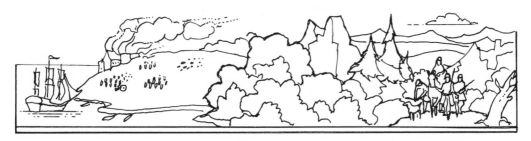

Ballad of Johnny Appleseed

Through the Appalachian valleys,
  with his kit a buckskin bag,
Johnny Appleseed went plodding
  past high peak and mountain
  crag.
Oh, his stockings were of leather,
  and his moccasins were tough;
He was set upon a journey where the
  going would be rough.
  See him coming in the
  springtime,
  Passing violets in the glade.
  Many apple trees are needed,
  And the pioneers want shade.
Johnny carried many orchards in the
  bag upon his back,
And the scent of apple blossoms
  always lingered in his track.
Over half a fertile continent he
  planted shiny seed;
He would toss them in the clearings
  where the fawn and yearling
  feed.
  In the summer see him tramping
  Through the windings of the
  wood.
  Big red apples in the oven
  Make the venison taste good.
He would wander over mountain;
  he would brave a raging
  stream,
For his eyes were filled with visions
  like an ancient prophet's
  dream.
He would travel after nightfall, start
  again at early morn;
He was planting seeds of apples for
  the children yet unborn.
  Where the autumn leaves
  turned crimson,
  He was eager to explore.

Apple dumplings never
  blossomed
On a shady sycamore.
Johnny traveled where the war
  whoop of the painted tribes
  rang loud;
And he walked among grim
  chieftains and their hot-eyed
  warrior crowd.
He told them of his vision, of his
  dream that would not die,
So he never was molested, and the
  settlers had their pie.
  Bitter winter found him trudging,
  Not for glory or applause,
  Only happy for the winesaps
  In tomorrow's applesauce!

Helmer O. Oleson

These are the times that try men's
souls. The summer soldier and the
sunshine patriot will, in this crisis,
shrink from the service of their country; but he that stands it *now*, de-
serves the love and thanks of man
and woman. Tyranny, like hell, is
not easily conquered; yet we have
this consolation with us, that the
harder the conflict, the more glorious the triumph. What we obtain too
cheap, we esteem too lightly; 'tis
dearness only that gives everything
its value. Heaven knows how to put
a proper price upon its goods; and it
would be strange, indeed, if so celes-
tial an article as *Freedom* should not
be highly rated.

Thomas Paine
(from The American Crisis)

The Gettysburg Address

Fourscore and seven years ago our fathers brought forth on this continent, a new nation,

Conceived in Liberty, and dedicated to the proposition that all men are created equal.

Now we are engaged in a great civil war, testing whether that nation or any nation so conceived and so dedicated can long endure.

We are met on a great battlefield of that war.

We have come to dedicate a portion of that field, as a final resting place for those who here gave their lives that that nation might live.

It is altogether fitting and proper that we should do this.

But, in a larger sense, we cannot dedicate — we cannot consecrate — we cannot hallow — this ground.

The brave men, living and dead, who struggled here, have consecrated it far above our poor power to add or detract.

The world will little note nor long remember what we say here,

But it can never forget what they did here.

It is for us, the living, rather to be dedicated here to the unfinished work which they who fought here have thus far so nobly advanced.

It is rather for us to be here dedicated to the great task remaining before us —

That from these honored dead we take increased devotion to that cause for which they gave the last full measure of devotion;

That we here highly resolve that these dead shall not have died in vain;

That this nation, under God, shall have a new birth of freedom;

And that government of the people, by the people, for the people,

Shall not perish from the earth.

Abraham Lincoln

Ten Rules of Conduct for Individuals and Nations

1. You cannot bring about prosperity by discouraging thrift.
2. You cannot strengthen the weak by weakening the strong.
3. You cannot help small men by tearing down big men.
4. You cannot help the wage earner by pulling down the wage payer.
5. You cannot further the brotherhood of many by encouraging class hatred.
6. You cannot help the poor by destroying the rich.
7. You cannot establish sound security on borrowed money.
8. You cannot keep out of trouble by spending more than you earn.
9. You cannot build character and courage by taking away man's initiative and independence.
10. You cannot help men permanently by doing for them what they could and should do for themselves.

Abraham Lincoln

Tribute to Robert E. Lee

He was a foe without hate,
  a friend without treachery,
  a soldier without cruelty, and
  a victim without murmuring.
He was a public officer without
     vices,
  a private citizen without wrong,
  a neighbor without reproach,
  a Christian without hypocrisy,
    and
  a man without guilt.
He was Caesar without his
    ambition,
  Frederick without his tyranny,
  Napoleon without his selfishness,
    and
  Washington without his reward.

Benjamin H. Hill

Old Ironsides

Ay, tear her tattered ensign down!
  Long has it waved on high,
And many an eye has danced to see
  That banner in the sky;
Beneath it rung the battle shout,
  And burst the cannon's roar:
The meteor of the ocean air
  Shall sweep the clouds no more!

Her decks, once red with heroes'
    blood,
  Where knelt the vanquished foe,
When winds were hurrying o'er the
    flood
  And waves were white below,
No more shall feel the victor's tread,
  Or know the conquered knee:
The harpies of the shore shall pluck
  The eagle of the sea!

O better that her shattered hulk
  Should sink beneath the wave!
Her thunders shook the mighty
    deep,
  And there should be her grave:
Nail to the mast her holy flag,
  Set every threadbare sail,
And give her to the god of storms,
  The lightning and the gale!

Oliver Wendell Holmes

The Cowboy's Life

The bawl of a steer
To a cowboy's ear
Is music of sweetest strain;
And the yelping notes
Of the gay coyotes
To him are a glad refrain.

For a kingly crown
In the noisy town
His saddle he wouldn't change;
No life so free
As the life we see
Way out on the Yaso range.

The rapid beat
Of his broncho's feet
On the sod as he speeds along,
Keeps living time
To the ringing rhyme
Of his rollicking cowboy song.

The winds may blow
And the thunder growl
Or the breezes may safely moan;
A cowboy's life
Is a royal life,
His saddle his kingly throne.

Attributed to James Barton Adams

156

Casey Jones

Come all you rounders that want to
    hear
A story about a brave engineer;
Casey Jones was the hogger's name.
On the Western Pacific he won his
    fame.

The caller called Casey at half-past
    four.
He kissed his wife at the station
    door.
He mounted to the cabin with his
    orders in his hand,
And took his farewell journey to the
    Promised Land.

Put in your water and shovel on your
    coal,
Stick your head out the window, and
    watch her roll.
We've got to run her till she leaves
    the rail,
For we're eight hours late with the
    Western Mail.

Casey looked at his watch, and his
    watch was slow.
He looked at the water, and the
    water was low.
He turned to the fireman, and
    "Boy," he said,
"We've got to reach Frisco, or we'll
    all be dead."

Casey pulled up on Reno Hill,
And tooted on the whistle with an
    awful shrill.
The crossing man knew by the
    engine's moans
That the man at the throttle was
    Casey Jones.

Casey pulled up within two miles of
    the place,
With Number Four staring him right
    in the face.
He turned to the fireman, said,
    "Boy, you'd better jump,
For there's two locomotives that's
    going to bump."

Casey said just before he died,
"There's two more roads that I'd like
    to ride."
The fireman said, "What may they
    be?"
"Why, the Southern Pacific and the
    Santa Fe."

In Flanders Fields

In Flanders fields the poppies blow
Between the crosses, row on row,
    That mark our place; and in the
      sky
    The larks, still bravely singing, fly
Scarce heard amid the guns below.

We are the Dead. Short days ago
We lived, felt dawn, saw sunset
    glow,
    Loved and were loved, and now
      we lie
    In Flanders fields.

Take up our quarrel with the foe:
To you from failing hands we throw
    The torch; be yours to hold it high.
    If ye break faith with us who die
We shall not sleep, though poppies
    grow
    In Flanders fields.

John McCrae

157

God Bless America

God bless America,
    Land that I love,
Stand beside her and guide her
    Through the night with the light
      from above.
From the mountains, to the prairies,
    To the ocean white with foam,
God bless America,
    My home sweet home,
God bless America,
    My home sweet home.

Irving Berlin

Battle Hymn of the Republic

Mine eyes have seen the glory of the
    coming of the Lord;
He is trampling out the vintage
    where the grapes of wrath are
    stored;
He hath loosed the fateful lightning
    of His terrible swift sword;
His truth is marching on.

I have seen Him in the watch-fires of
    a hundred circling camps;
They have builded Him an altar in
    the evening dews and damps;
I can read His righteous sentence by
    the dim and flaring lamps;
His day is marching on.

I have read a fiery gospel, writ in
    burnish'd rows of steel;
"As ye deal with My contemners, so
    with you My grace shall deal;
Let the Hero, born of woman, crush
    the serpent with His heel,
Since God is marching on."

He has sounded forth the trumpet
    that shall never call retreat;
He is sifting out the hearts of men
    before His judgment-seat:
O be swift, my soul, to answer
    Him! be jubilant, my feet!
Our God is marching on.

In the beauty of the lilies Christ
    was born across the sea,
With a glory in His bosom that
    transfigures you and me:
As He died to make men holy, let us
    die to make men free,
While God is marching on.

Glory! Glory! Hallelujah!
Glory! Glory! Hallelujah!
Glory! Glory! Hallelujah!
His truth is marching on.

Julia Ward Howe

America

My country, 'tis of thee,
Sweet land of liberty,
Of thee I sing;
Land where my fathers died,
Land of the pilgrims' pride,
From every mountain side
Let freedom ring!

My native country, thee,
Land of the noble free,
Thy name I love;
I love thy rocks and rills,
Thy woods and templed hills;
My heart with rapture thrills,
Like that above.

Let music swell the breeze,
And ring from all the trees
Sweet freedom's song;
Let mortal tongues awake;
Let all that breathe partake;
Let rocks their silence break,
The sound prolong.

Our fathers' God, to Thee,
Author of liberty,
To Thee we sing;
Long may our land be bright
With freedom's holy light;
Protect us by Thy might,
Great God, our King!

Samuel F. Smith

Columbia, the Gem of the Ocean

O Columbia, the gem of the ocean,
  The home of the brave and the
    free,
The shrine of each patriot's
    devotion,
  A world offers homage to thee.
Thy mandates make heroes
    assemble,
  When Liberty's form stands in
    view;
Thy banners make tyranny tremble,
  When borne by the red, white,
    and blue.

When borne by the red, white, and
  blue,
When borne by the red, white, and
  blue;
Thy banners make tyranny tremble,
When borne by the red, white, and
  blue.

Thomas A. Becket

Abraham Lincoln's Creed

I believe in God, the Almighty Ruler
of nations, our great and good and
merciful Maker, our Father in
heaven, who notes the fall of a sparrow and numbers the hairs on our
heads. I recognize the sublime truth
announced in the Holy Scriptures
and proved by all history that those
nations are blessed whose God is the
Lord. I believe that the will of God
prevails. Without him, all human re-
liance is vain. With that assistance I
cannot fail. I have a solemn vow re-
gistered in heaven to finish the work
I am in, in full view of my responsi-
bility to my God, with malice toward
none; with charity for all; with
firmness in the right, as God gives
me to see the right.

Compiled by William E. Barton

America the Beautiful

O beautiful for spacious skies,
  For amber waves of grain,
For purple mountain majesties
  Above the fruited plain!
    America! America!
  God shed His grace on thee
And crown thy good with
    brotherhood
  From sea to shining sea!

O beautiful for pilgrim feet,
  Whose stern, impassioned stress
A thoroughfare for freedom beat
  Across the wilderness!
    America! America!
  God mend thine every flaw,
Confirm thy soul in self-control,
  Thy liberty in law!

O beautiful for heroes proved
  In liberating strife,
Who more than self their country
    loved,
  And mercy more than life!
    America! America!
  May God thy gold refine,
Till all success be nobleness
  And every gain divine!

O beautiful for patriot dream
  That sees beyond the years
Thine alabaster cities gleam
  Undimmed by human tears!
    America! America!
  God shed His grace on thee
And crown thy good with
    brotherhood
  From sea to shining sea!

Katharine Lee Bates

159

Patriotism

Breathes there a man, with soul so
    dead,
Who never to himself hath said,
  This is my own, my native land!
Whose heart hath ne'er within him
    burned,
As home his footsteps he hath
    turned,
    From wandering on a foreign
     strand!
If such there breathe, go, mark him
    well;
For him no Minstrel raptures swell;
High though his titles, proud his
    name,
Boundless his wealth as wish can
    claim;
Despite those titles, power, and pelf,
The wretch, concentred all in self,
Living, shall forfeit fair renown,
And, doubly dying, shall go down
To the vile dust, from whence he
    sprung,
Unwept, unhonoured, and unsung.

Sir Walter Scott
(from The Lay of the Last Minstrel)

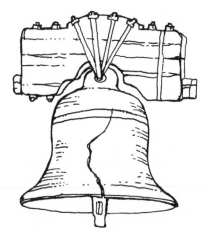

Preamble to the Constitution of the United States

We the people of the United States, in order to form a more perfect Union, establish justice, insure domestic tranquillity, provide for the common defense, promote the general welfare, and secure the blessings of liberty to ourselves and our posterity, do ordain and establish this Constitution for the United States of America.

Whenever I Say "America"

Whenever I say "America"
I say so many things! —
Something shouts in the syllables,
Something echoes and sings.
Maybe it's hope, maybe it's pride,
Maybe it's only love,
Maybe it's just a kind of hail
To the flag that flies above,
The flag that flies so broad and
    bright
From dawn to setting sun,
And takes the wind and takes the
    light, —
The flag our fathers won!

Whenever I say "America"
Old pictures come to me
Of lonely prows, slow pushing on
Across a stormy sea;
Of men and women who knew no
    rest,
Toiling with heart and hand,
Of covered wagons rocking west
Into an unknown land;
Of free men striving, striving still
In freedom's old, hard way . . .
Whenever I say "America"
So many things I say!

Nancy Byrd Turner

Preamble to the
Declaration of Independence

When, in the course of human events, it becomes necessary for one people to dissolve the political bands which have connected them with another, and to assume among the powers of the earth the separate and equal station to which the laws of nature and of nature's God entitle them, a decent respect to the opinions of mankind requires that they should declare the causes which impel them to the separation. We hold these truths to be self-evident; that all men are created equal; that they are endowed by their creator with certain unalienable rights; that among these are life, liberty, and the pursuit of happiness; that to secure these rights, governments are instituted among men, deriving their just powers from the consent of the governed; that whenever any form of government becomes destructive to these ends, it is the right of the people to alter or to abolish it, and to institute a new government, laying its foundation on such principles, and organizing its powers in such form, as to them shall seem most likely to effect their safety and happiness. Prudence, indeed, will dictate that governments long established should not be changed for light and transient causes; and accordingly all experience hath shown that mankind are more disposed to suffer, while evils are sufferable, than to right themselves by abolishing the forms to which they are accustomed.

Thomas Jefferson

Our Wonderful World

How could God think of so many
    kinds of houses?
There are millions of houses that I
    can't even see.
There must be lots of very funny
    ones!
  Mole houses —
      Frog houses —
          Beaver houses —
  Stork nests on chimneys,
  Squirrel nests in trees.
  Houses for everyone!
    And my house
      for me.

Jessie Orton Jones
(XXI from Secrets)

The Wonderful World

Great, wide, beautiful, wonderful
World,
With the wonderful water round you
curled,
And the wonderful grass upon your
breast,
World, you are beautifully dressed.

The wonderful air is over me,
And the wonderful wind is shaking
the tree —
It walks on the water, and whirls the
mills,
And talks to itself on the top of the
hills.

You friendly Earth, how far do you
go,
With the wheat fields that nod and
the rivers that flow,
With cities and gardens and cliffs
and isles,
And the people upon you for
thousands of miles?

Ah! you are so great, and I am so
small,
I hardly can think of you, World, at
all;
And yet, when I said my prayers
today,
My mother kissed me, and said,
quite gay,

"If the wonderful World is great to
you,
And great to Father and Mother, too,
You are more than the Earth, though
you are such a dot!
You can love and think, and the
Earth cannot!"

William Brighty Rands

The Wind

I saw you toss the kites on high
And blow the birds about the sky;
And all around I heard you pass,
Like ladies' skirts across the grass —
  O wind, a-blowing all day long,
  O wind, that sings so loud a song!

I saw the different things you did,
But always you yourself you hid.
I felt you push, I heard you call,
I could not see yourself at all —
  O wind, a-blowing all day long,
  O wind, that sings so loud a song!

Robert Louis Stevenson

Little Wind

Little wind, blow on the hilltop,
Little wind, blow on the plain,
Little wind, blow up the sunshine,
Little wind, blow off the rain.

Who Has Seen the Wind?

Who has seen the wind?
  Neither I nor you:
But when the leaves hang trembling
  The wind is passing thro'.

Who has seen the wind?
  Neither you nor I:
But when the trees bow down their
  heads
  The wind is passing by.

Christina Rossetti

The Wind

The wind stood up, and gave a
    shout;
He whistled on his fingers, and

Kicked the withered leaves about,
And thumped the branches with his
    hand,

And said he'd kill, and kill, and kill;
And so he will! And so he will!

James Stephens

O, Look at the Moon

O, look at the moon,
    She is shining up there;
O, mother, she looks
    Like a lamp in the air.

Last week she was smaller,
    And shaped like a bow,
But now she's grown bigger,
    And round like an O.

The Star

Twinkle, twinkle, little star,
How I wonder what you are!
Up above the world so high,
Like a diamond in the sky.

As your bright and tiny spark
Lights the traveler in the dark,
Though I know not what you are,
Twinkle, twinkle, little star.

Jane Taylor

I see the moon,
And the moon sees me;
God bless the moon,
And God bless me.

The Universe

There is the moon, there is the sun
Round which we circle every year,
And there are all the stars we see
On starry nights when skies are
    clear,
And all the countless stars that lie
Beyond the reach of human eye.
If every bud on every tree,
All birds and fireflies and bees,
And all the flowers that bloom and
    die,
Upon the earth were counted up,
The number of the stars would be
Greater, they say, than all of these.

Mary Britton Miller

Things We Can Depend On

The sun is gone down,
    And the moon's in the sky;
But the sun will come up,
    And the moon be laid by.
The flower is asleep,
    But it is not dead;
When the morning shines,
    It will lift up its head.

George MacDonald

The Song of the Brook

I come from haunts of coot and hern,
  I make a sudden sally,
And sparkle out among the fern,
  To bicker down a valley.

By thirty hills I hurry down,
  Or slip between the ridges,
By twenty thorps, a little town,
  And half a hundred bridges.

Till last by Philip's farm I flow
  To join the brimming river;
For men may come, and men may
    go,
  But I go on forever.

I chatter over stony ways,
  In little sharps and trebles;
I bubble into eddying bays,
  I babble on the pebbles.

With many a curve my bank I fret
  By many a field and fallow,
And many a fairy foreland set
  With willow-weed and mallow.

I chatter, chatter, as I flow
  To join the brimming river;
For men may come, and men may
    go,
  But I go on forever.

I wind about, and in and out,
  With here a blossom sailing,
And here and there a lusty trout,
  And here and there a grayling,

And here and there a foamy flake
  Upon me as I travel,
With many a silvery waterbreak
  Above the golden gravel,

And draw them all along and flow
  To join the brimming river;
For men may come, and men may
    go,
  But I go on forever.

I steal by lawns and grassy plots,
  I slide by hazel covers,
I move the sweet forget-me-nots
  That grow for happy lovers.

I slip, I slide, I gloom, I glance,
  Among my skimming swallows;
I make the netted sunbeam dance
  Against my sandy shallows.

I murmur under moon and stars
  In brambly wildernesses;
I linger by my shingly bars,
  I loiter round my cresses;

And out again I curve and flow
  To join the brimming river;
For men may come, and men may
    go,
  But I go on forever.

Alfred Tennyson

The Handiwork of God

I believe in the brook as it wanders
  From hillside into glade;
I believe in the breeze as it whispers
  When evening shadows fade.
I believe in the roar of the river
  As it dashes from high cascade;
I believe in the cry of the tempest
  'Mid the thunder's cannonade.
I believe in the light of the shining
    stars,
  I believe in the sun and the moon;
I believe in the flash of the lightning,
  I believe in the nightbird's croon.
I believe in the faith of the flowers,
  I believe in the rock and the sod,
For in all of these appeareth clear
  The handiwork of God.

Happy Thought

The world is so full of a number of
    things,
I'm sure we should all be as happy as
    kings.

Robert Louis Stevenson

I Saw Some Lovely Things Today

I saw some lovely things today:
I feel, dear God, I'd like to pray.
I saw some tiny, little things —
Some hummingbirds with gauzy
    wings,
A flower with its head held high
As though its blue came from the
    sky.
I saw some lovely things today:
I feel, dear God, I'd like to pray.

I heard some wondrous things
    today:
I feel, dear God, I'd like to pray.
I heard a brook. It seemed to me
To catch the rhythm of the sea.
I heard a bird. It sang to me
A joyous, lilting melody.
I heard some wondrous things
    today:
I feel, dear God, I'd like to pray.

Perhaps, dear Lord, the woodland
    air
Was really breathing out a prayer —
    The prayer I prayed.
The awe and wonder in my heart
Were such a very vital part
    Of what thou callest prayer.

Thanatopsis

To him who in the love of Nature
    holds
Communion with her visible forms,
    she speaks
A various language; for his gayer
    hours
She has a voice of gladness, and a
    smile
And eloquence of beauty, and she
    glides
Into his darker musings, with a mild
And healing sympathy, that steals
    away
Their sharpness, ere he is aware.

William Cullen Bryant

The Creator

The earth *is* the Lord's, and the
    fulness thereof;
    the world, and they that dwell
        therein.
For he hath founded it upon the
    seas,
    and established it upon the floods.
Who shall ascend into the hill of the
    Lord?
    or who shall stand in his holy
        place?
He that hath clean hands, and a pure
    heart;
    who hath not lifted up his soul
        unto vanity,
    nor sworn deceitfully.
He shall receive the blessing from
    the Lord,
    and righteousness from the God of
        his salvation.
This is the generation of them that
    seek him,
    that seek thy face, O Jacob.
Lift up your heads, O ye gates;
And be ye lifted up, ye everlasting
    doors;
    and the King of glory shall come
        in.
Who is this King of glory?
The Lord strong and mighty,
The Lord mighty in battle.
Lift up your heads, O ye gates;
Even lift them up, ye everlasting
    doors;
    and the King of glory shall come
        in.
Who is this King of glory?
The Lord of hosts,
He *is* the King of glory.

The Bible, Psalm 24

Praise to God for things we see —
Growing grass, the waving tree,
Mother's face, the bright, blue sky,
Birds and clouds floating by.
Praise to God for things we see,
Praise to God for seeing.

M. M. Penstone

All Things Bright and Beautiful

All things bright and beautiful,
    All creatures great and small,
All things wise and wonderful,
    The Lord God made them all.

Each little flower that opens,
    Each little bird that sings,
God made their glowing colors,
    He made their tiny wings.

The purple-headed mountain,
    The river running by,
The sunset, and the morning
    That brightens up the sky.

The cold wind in the winter,
    The pleasant summer sun,
The ripe fruits in the garden —
    He made them every one.

The tall trees in the greenwood,
    The meadows where we play,
The rushes by the water,
    We gather every day.

He gave us eyes to see them,
    And lips that we might tell
How great is God Almighty,
    Who doeth all things well.

Cecil Frances Alexander

Rain

The rain is raining all around,
    It falls on field and tree,
It rains on the umbrellas here,
    And on the ships at sea.

Robert Louis Stevenson

This Is My Father's World

This is my Father's world,
    And to my listening ears,
All nature sings, and round me rings
    The music of the spheres.
This is my Father's world
    I rest me in the thought
Of rocks and trees, of skies and seas;
    His hand the wonders wrought.

This is my Father's world,
The birds their carols raise,
The morning light, the lily white,
    Declare their Maker's praise.
This is my Father's world:
    He shines in all that's fair;
In the rustling grass I hear Him pass,
    He speaks to me everywhere.

This is my Father's world,
    O let me ne'er forget
That though the wrong seems oft so
        strong,
    God is the Ruler yet.
This is my Father's world:
    The battle is not done;
Jesus who died shall be satisfied,
    And earth and heaven be one.

Maltbie D. Babcock

Fog

The fog comes
on little cat feet.

It sits looking
over harbor and city
on silent haunches
and then moves on.

Carl Sandburg

Oh, Who Can Make a Flower?

Oh, who can make a flower?
I'm sure I can't. Can you?
Oh, who can make a flower?
No one but God — 'tis true.

Oh, who can make the sunshine?
I'm sure I can't. Can you?
Oh, who can make the raindrops?
No one but God — 'tis true.

Grace W. Owens

Great Is the Lord

Praise ye the Lord:
For it is good to sing praises
   unto our God;
For it is pleasant; and praise
   is comely.
Great is our Lord, and of great
   power:
Who covereth the heaven with
   clouds,
Who prepareth rain for the earth,
Who maketh grass to grow upon the
   mountains.
He giveth to the beast his food,
And to the young ravens which cry.
He giveth snow like wool:
He scattereth the hoarfrost like
   ashes.
He casteth forth his ice like morsels:
Who can stand before his cold?
He sendeth out his word, and
   melteth them:
He causeth his wind to blow, and
   the waters flow.
Sing unto the Lord with
   thanksgiving;
Praise ye the Lord.

The Bible, Psalm 147:1,5,8,9,
16-18,7,20

I'm glad the sky is painted blue;
And the earth is painted green;
And such a lot of nice fresh air
All sandwiched in between.

Baby Seeds

In a milkweed cradle,
Snug and warm,
Baby seeds are hiding,
Safe from harm.
Open wide the cradle,
Hold it high!
Come Mr. Wind,
Help them fly.

The heavens declare the glory of
   God;
   and the firmament sheweth his
      handywork.
Day unto day uttereth speech,
   and night unto night sheweth
      knowledge.
There is no speech nor language,
   where their voice is not heard.
Their line is gone out through all the
   earth,
   and their words to the end of the
      world.
In them hath he set a tabernacle for
   the sun,
Which is as a bridegroom coming
   out of his chamber,
   and rejoiceth as a strong man to
      run a race.
His going forth is from the end of the
   heaven,
   and his circuit unto the ends of it:
And there is nothing hid from the
   heat thereof.

The Bible, Psalm 19:1-6

Silver

Slowly, silently, now the moon
Walks the night in her silver shoon;
This way, and that, she peers, and
   sees
Silver fruit upon silver trees;
One by one the casements catch
Her beams beneath the silvery
   thatch;
Couched in his kennel, like a log,
With paws of silver sleeps the dog;
From their shadowy cote the white
   breasts peep
Of doves in a silver-feathered sleep;
A harvest mouse goes scampering
   by,
With silver claws, and silver eye;
And moveless fish in the water
   gleam,
By silver reeds in a silver stream.

Walter de la Mare

Rules to Live By

Lay not up for yourselves treasures
    upon earth,
Where moth and rust doth corrupt,
And where thieves break through
    and steal:

But lay up for yourselves treasures in
    heaven,
Where neither moth nor rust doth
    corrupt,
And where thieves do not break
    through nor steal:

For where your treasure is, there will
    your heart be also.

The Bible, Matthew 6:19-21

Grizzly Bear

If you ever, ever, ever meet a grizzly
    bear,
You must never, never, never ask
    him *where*
He is going,
Or *what* he is doing;
For if you ever, ever dare
To stop a grizzly bear
You will never meet *another* grizzly
    bear.

Mary Austin

Seldom Can't

Seldom "can't,"
    Seldom "don't";
Never "shan't,"
    Never "won't."

Christina Rossetti

Go to bed late
    Stay very small;
Go to bed early
    Grow very tall.

Today I lost my temper,
    And angry words were said:
Words that did not help at all,
And they are now beyond recall —
    The angry words I said.

Good and Bad

There is so much good in the worst
    of us,
And so much bad in the best of us,
That it hardly becomes any of us
To talk about the rest of us.

Edward Wallis Hoch

Always Finish

If a task is once begun,
Never leave it till it's done.
Be the labor great or small,
Do it well or not at all.

Early to bed, early to rise
Makes a man healthy, wealthy, and
    wise.

An acre of performance is worth a
whole world of promise.

Thomas James Howell

A Bit of the Book

A bit of the Book* in the morning,
    To order my onward way.
A bit of the Book in the evening,
    To hallow the end of the day.

Margaret E. Sangster

* Bible

Fret Not

Fret not thyself because of
    evildoers,
Neither be thou envious against the
    workers of iniquity.
For they shall soon be cut down like
    the grass,
And wither as the green herb.
I have seen the wicked in great
    power,
And spreading himself like a green
    bay tree.
Yet he passed away, and, lo, he was
    not:
Yea, I sought him, but he could not
    be found.
Trust in the Lord, and do good;
So shalt thou dwell in the land,
And verily thou shalt be fed.

The Bible, Psalm 37:1,2,35,36,3

In everything you do
Aim to excel,
For what's worth doing
Is worth doing well.

My son, forget not my law; but let
thine heart keep my command-
ments;
For length of days, and long life,
and peace, shall they add to thee.
Let not mercy and truth forsake
thee: bind them about thy neck;
write them upon the table of thine
heart:
So shalt thou find favour and good
understanding in the sight of God
and man.

The Bible, Proverbs 3:1–4

Whatsoever things are true,
Whatsoever things are honest,
Whatsoever things are just,
Whatsoever things are pure,
Whatsoever things are lovely,
Whatsoever things are of
      good report;
If there be any virtue,
And if there be any praise,
Think on these things.

The Bible, Philippians 4:8

John Wesley's Rule

Do all the good you can,
In all the ways you can,
In all the places you can,
At all the times you can,
To all the people you can,
As long as ever you can.

Be ye kind one to another.

The Bible, Ephesians 4:32

Be kindly affectioned one to
another with brotherly love; in
honor preferring one another; not
slothful in business; fervent in
spirit; serving the Lord.

The Bible, Romans 12:10,11

Short Sermon

To give — and forgive —
Is a good way to live.

*Adapted from the German by
Louis Untermeyer*

173

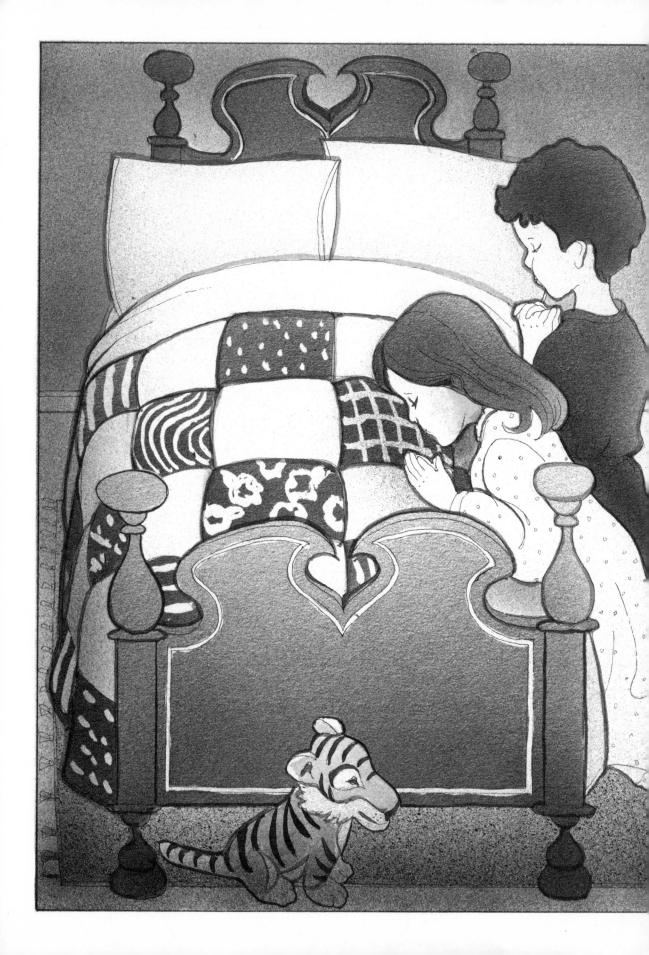

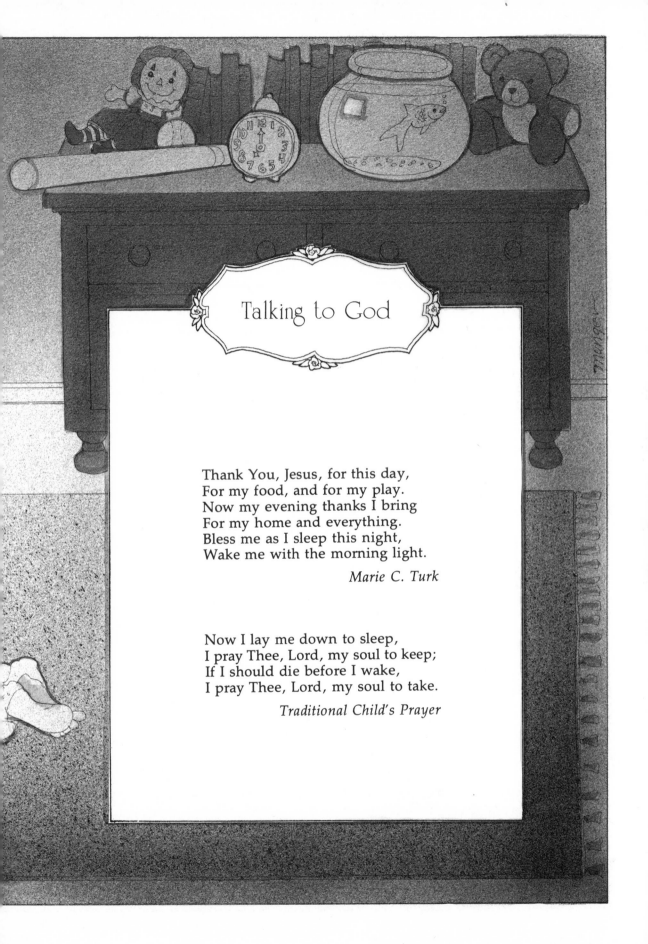

Talking to God

Thank You, Jesus, for this day,
For my food, and for my play.
Now my evening thanks I bring
For my home and everything.
Bless me as I sleep this night,
Wake me with the morning light.

Marie C. Turk

Now I lay me down to sleep,
I pray Thee, Lord, my soul to keep;
If I should die before I wake,
I pray Thee, Lord, my soul to take.

Traditional Child's Prayer

The Lord's Prayer

Our Father which art in heaven,
Hallowed be thy name.
Thy kingdom come.
Thy will be done
   in earth, as it is in heaven.

Give us this day
   our daily bread.
And forgive us our debts,
   as we forgive our debtors.
And lead us not into temptation,
   but deliver us from evil:

For thine is the kingdom,
   and the power,
   and the glory,
   for ever. Amen.

The Bible, Matthew 6:9-13

It's Me Again, God

I come every day
Just to talk with You, Lord,
And to learn how to pray . . .
You make me feel welcome,
You reach out Your hand,
I need never explain
For YOU understand . . .
I come to You frightened
And burdened with care
So lonely and lost
And so filled with despair,
And suddenly, Lord,
I'm no longer afraid,
My burden is lighter
And the dark shadows fade . . .
Oh, God, what a comfort
To know that You care
And to know when I seek You
YOU WILL ALWAYS BE THERE!

Helen Steiner Rice

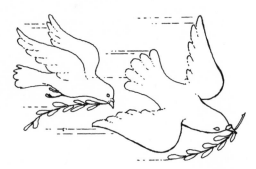

Thanks

Dear Lord, we give Thee thanks for
   the bright silent moon
And thanks for the sun that will
   warm us at noon.
And thanks for the stars and the
   quick running breeze,
And thanks for the shade and
   the straightness of trees.

Prayer

Prayer is so simple
It is like quietly opening a door
And slipping into the very presence
   of God,
There in the stillness
To listen for his voice.
Perhaps to petition
Or only to listen,
It matters not;
Just to be there,
In his presence,
Is prayer!

Give Thanks

Oh, give thanks to Him who made
Morning light and evening shade;
Source and giver of all good,
Nightly sleep, and daily food,
Quickener of our wearied powers;
Guard of our unconscious hours.

A Simple Prayer

Lord, make me an instrument of
    Your peace.
Where there is hatred . . .
    Let me sow love;
Where there is injury . . .
    Pardon;
Where there is doubt . . .
    Faith;
Where there is despair . . .
    Hope;
Where there is darkness . . .
    Light;
Where there is sadness . . .
    Joy.

O Divine Master, grant that I may
    Not so much seek
To be consoled . . .
    As to console;
To be understood . . .
    As to understand,
To be loved . . .
    As to love, for
It is in giving that we receive,
It is in pardoning that we are
    pardoned,
It is in dying that we are born to
    eternal life.

St. Francis of Assisi

The Christian's Prayer

Lord, make me free . . .
    From fear of the future;
    From anxiety of the morrow;
    From bitterness toward anyone;
    From cowardice in face of danger;
    From failure before opportunity;
    From laziness in face of work.

My Savior, Hear My Prayer

My Savior, hear my prayer
Before I go to rest;
It is Your little child
Who comes now to be blest.

Forgive me all my sin,
And let me sleep this night
In safety and in peace
Until the morning light.

Henry L. Jenner

A Thought

It is very nice to think
The world is full of
    meat and drink,
With little children
    saying grace
In every Christian kind of place.

Robert Louis Stevenson

My Choice

Lord, may it be my choice
    This blessed rule to keep —
"Rejoice with them that do rejoice,
    And weep with those that weep."

Each prayer is answered,
That is so;
But for our good
It may be, "No!"

Prayer for a Pilot

Lord of Sea and Earth and Air,
Listen to the Pilot's prayer —
Send him wind that's steady and
  strong,
Grant that his engine sings the song
Of flawless tone, by which he knows
It shall not fail him where he goes;
Landing, gliding, in curve,
  half-roll —
Grant him, O Lord, a full control,
That he may learn in heights of
  Heaven
The rapture altitude has given,
That he shall know the joy they feel
Who ride Thy realms on Birds of
  Steel.

Cecil Roberts

A Prayer for Love

I pray for a child-like heart,
  For gentle, holy love,
For strength to do Thy will below,
  As angels do above.
On friends to me most dear,
  Oh, let Thy blessing fall;
I pray for grace to love them well,
  But Thee beyond them all.

An Evening Prayer

Now I lay me down to sleep,
I pray Thee, Lord, Thy child to keep;
Thy love go with me all the night
And wake me with the morning
  light.

Night Blessing

Good night
Sleep tight
Wake up bright
In the morning light
To do what's right
With all your might.

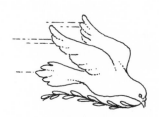

A Prayer

Teach me, Father, how to go
Softly as the grasses grow;
Hush my soul to meet the shock
Of the wild world as a rock;
But my spirit, propt with power,
Make as simple as a flower.
Let the dry heart fill its cup,
Like a poppy looking up;
Let life lightly wear her crown,
Like a poppy looking down,
When its heart is filled with dew,
And its life begins anew.

Teach me, Father, how to be
Kind and patient as a tree.
Joyfully the crickets croon
Under shady oak at noon;
Beetle, on his mission bent,
Tarries in that cooling tent.
Let me, also, cheer a spot,
Hidden field or garden grot —
Placed where passing souls can rest
On the way and be their best.

Edwin Markham

God, Are You There?

I'm way down HERE!
You're way up THERE!
Are You sure You can hear
My faint, faltering prayer?
For I'm so unsure
Of just how to pray —
To tell you the truth, God,
I don't know what to say . . .
I just know I am lonely
And vaguely disturbed,
Bewildered and restless,
Confused and perturbed . . .
And they tell me that prayer
Helps to quiet the mind
And to unburden the heart,
For in stillness we find
A newborn assurance
That SOMEONE DOES CARE
And SOMEONE DOES ANSWER
Each small sincere prayer!

Helen Steiner Rice

Grace for a Child

Here a little child I stand,
Heaving up my either hand;
Cold as paddocks though they be,
Here I lift them up to Thee,
For a benison* to fall
On our meat and on us all,
                    Amen.

Robert Herrick
*blessing

179

Children Are Authors Too!

Come with me to the mushroom
    patch,
Where mushrooms grow, batch by
    batch.
But you must be careful, you shall
    see,
Not all of them are good for you and
    me.

The colorless plants of brown and
    white,
With the dew settling on them late at
    night,
Stand all alone like ghosts and
    spooks,
Friendless because others don't like
    their looks.

Sometimes you think of fairies and
    elves,
Using those mushrooms as their
    shelves.
But don't you believe in those fairy
    tales,
They're only written to increase
    sales.

(Tale of Mushrooms)
Lynda Hiott, Age 12

Rules to Live By

Never put anybody down.
Remember that everyone else is
    human, too.
Benefit from everything you do.
Last but not least, obey all other
    rules in life for a happy one.

Paula Del Giudice, Age 12

Blind but Happy

O what a happy soul am I!
    Although I cannot see,
I am resolved that in this world
    Contented I will be;
How many blessings I enjoy
    That other people don't!
To weep and sigh because I'm blind,
    I cannot and I won't.

Fanny Crosby
(written at Age 8)

Grandma

My grandma likes to play with God,
They have a kind of game.
She plants the garden full of seeds,
He sends the sun and rain.

She likes to sit and talk with God
And knows he is right there.
She prays about the whole wide
    world,
Then leaves us in his care.

Ann Johnson, Age 8

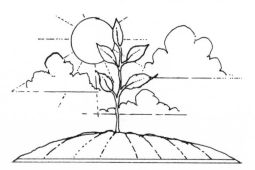

Rhapsodies

There are many things I love to hear
    Of things composed from this past
        year,
The sound of the trumpets, the beat
    of the snare,
    Of music happy and of great
        despair.
But of all the music I have ever
    known
    The rhapsodies that have grown
From the hearts of men so deep and
    still
    Of the power and strength of the
        musician's skill,
Seem to entrance me still
    Into a world of make believe:
Gershwin's Rhapsody in Blue
Chopin's Nocturne, Purple Hue
Beethoven's lovely Moonlight
    Sonata
And Wagner's lively Pitzue Contata
    All these and many more
Have taken the keys and unlocked
    the door
    To many a heart and many a mind
    Of many a person of many a kind.

Judy Turner, Age 13

Dear heavenly Father,
    Thank You for making
        everything,
    Thank You for making me so that
        I could grow up
        and grow old
        and die
        and go to heaven
        and see what You're like.
I can't see You, God,
    but You can see me! Amen.

Said at prayer time by Christian Holt,
Age 5, and recorded by his
grandmother, Mrs. Dixie Baer

Up on the Moon

T'was the night before Christmas,
    and up on the moon
Not a martian was stirring;
    It was a little past noon.
The stockings were hung in the
    crater with care,
In hopes that Santa would come
    right there.
The moon kids were nestled
    all snug in their beds,
And Mama in her craterchief,
    and I in my cap,
Had just settled down
    for a long moon nap,
When out on the moon dust
    arose such a clatter,
I sprang from my bed to see
    what was the matter.
But what to my martian eyes
    should appear,
But a tiny moon buggy and
    eight moondeer,
With a little old martian
    so lively and quick,
I knew in a moment it must be
    St. Nick.
And then in a second, I heard
    on the crater,
The stamping and stomping of hoofs
    grew much greater.
As I was slowly turning and
    glancing around,
Down the crater chimney he came
    with a bound.

He was dressed all in fur,
    from his head to his foot,
And his clothes were all covered
    with ashes and soot;
A bundle of toys he had
    on his back,
And he looked like a peddler
    just opening his pack.
He spoke not a word, but went
    straight to his work;
He filled all the stockings,
    then turned with a jerk,
Putting his head gear over
    his nose,
And with a nod up the crater
    chimney he rose;
He leaped to his moon buggy,
    to his moondeer gave a whistle,
And away they flew just as fast
    as a missile.
But I heard on the intercom as he
    drove out of sight,
"Merry Christmas to all and to all a
    Good Night!"

Nona Maiola, Age 12

I hear but my brain doesn't get the message.

Andrew Pacheco, Age 12

Definitions by Sixth Graders

A SIXTH GRADER is a person in the middle of growing up.

Sally Evans

ANGER is when someone is tired and emotional.

Mavis Harrison

LOVE is an understanding between two people who have certain feelings for each other and they get along because of it.

Tom Parmityr

PRAYER is talking to God to tell Him you love Him and believe in Him.

Carol Peterson

THE SKY is the seeable space around the earth. During the day it appears to be a blue dome surrounding the earth.

Blair West

A VACATION is a trip to get away from it all.

Terri Hall

WATER is what you drink when there isn't any soda pop.

Kirk Bradley

Do as you're told; don't argue.

Kelly Wignall, Age 12

Don't do unto others what you don't want them to do to you.

Stephanie Johnny, Age 13

The Soap Box Derby

When I was in a soap box derby,
I drove a car by the name of Herby.
 He had red wheels,
 I drove him through fields,
And I won the soap box derby!

Michael L. Kane, Age 10

The Man on the Moon

They say there's a man on the moon,
Who's due for a face-lifting soon.
 "The Russians," they say,
 "Will be there some day,
And wrinkle him up like a prune!"

Judy Turner, Age 10

Tips for Living

Never be rude.
Obey your elders.
Show love to all people
 even if they are not your friends.

Leandra Garcia, Age 11

Homework

Homework, homework,
Most monotonous kind of lone
 work!
I hate it when wanting to catch
 fishes,
But I love it when I should be doing
 dishes!

Gary Hoskins, Age 11

Mister Snowman

Look at Mr. Snowman
  Standing in the snow!
But when the sun is shining,
  He surely doesn't grow!
He gets a little shorter,
  With every passing hour,
But where he gently faded,
  Will grow a little flower.

Joleen Urriola, Age 11

Pioneers

These pioneers of olden days,
  With their sure and honest ways,
Helped the people, rich or poor,
  Only to give and help some more.

Clara Barton was one of those;
  She helped all, not a few she
    chose.
She nursed the soldiers, one by one,
  And didn't stop till she was done.

Benjamin Franklin worked and
    wrote,
  Made his stories, note by note.
He worked hard in the printing
    shops,
  Until of writers, he was "tops."

Marie Curie tried and tried,
  She worked on radium until she
    died.
Then she saw that glowing light
  In radium, that made life bright.

Ann Harris, Age 11

Owls

Some owls have big eyes,
And some have small,
But the owls with big eyes
See best of all!

Bob Merkel, Age 13

A Thanksgiving Prayer

On Thanksgiving Day, I'll say a little
    prayer,
To thank our heavenly Father for
    things so rare:
For our parents, kind and dear,
For our friends both far and near,
For the food that helps us grow,
For the rain and for the snow.
All these things I'm thankful for,
Yes, all of these and many more.

Kristy Woodward, Age 11

The Report Card

Violets are blue, roses are red;
Report cards are the one thing I
    dread!
One look at my card and lo and
    behold,
I should have done my work as I was
    told!

Richard Barrows, Age 11

Spring

I saw a bird high in the tree,
He was singing a song to me.
He sang, "Nothing can go wrong,
When I sing my happy song!"
He was as happy as could be,
Away up high in his big tree.

Pat Brennen, Age 7

Definitions by Fourth Graders

TEACHERS are people that help you learn things that you don't know.

COURAGE is when you're going to get spanked and stand up to it.

PATRIOTISM is love and loyal support of your country.

HAPPINESS is when you're going to get spanked and you don't.

A FRIEND is someone that you have fun with and who helps you.

A FATHER is someone you like. He is your mother's husband and loves you and is the boss.

A MOTHER is a person who brought you into the world and loves you and cares for you.

A HOME is a house, but you live in it to make it a home.

Thanks for Hearing

For ears to hear Your outdoor
    music,
  We thank Thee, God.
For birds singing early in the
    morning
And crickets squeaking in our
    gardens at night,
  We thank Thee, God.
For the "drip-drip" of the rain,
The happy chatter of the brook,
The splash and roar of the waves,
  We thank Thee, God.
For the whisper and rustling of the
    leaves,
And sometimes the loud "who-o-o"
    of the wind,
  We thank Thee, God.
For the church bells that sing to us
On a quiet Sunday morning,
  We thank Thee, God.

Written by the children of the Primary Department, First Congregational Church, Bristol, Connecticut

A Mother

I'd like to be a mother,
A mother dear and sweet,
And I want some children,
To keep nice and neat.
I wouldn't want my children
To run and rob a bank.
If they become good grown-ups,
They'll have me to thank.
There are lots of things I want to do,
But more than any other,
When I'm all grown-up,
I want to be a mother.

Victoria C. Armuth, Age 9

Character is something a person has. It is what kind of person he is. Or it will point out some good or some bad thing you did not know about them.

Layne Felsted   Age 12

William Penn

William Penn owned millions of
    acres,
But he gave up a life of ease
To join his friends, the Quakers.

Our hero went to jail,
A dirty place, indeed.
Another man joined him,
His name was William Mead.

Penn went to the king, and said,
"Have mercy on our band,
We want a peaceful settlement in
Your wonderful new land."

William didn't have colorful things,
His clothes were not very showy,
But he always was able and ready,
In weather both clear and snowy.

From the Old Country,
England, they came.
They founded their own city,
Philadelphia was its name.

          Carol Harriman, Age 11

A Kite

If I were a kite, high in the sky,
I might see many types of birds go
    by.
Whenever my master tugged on the
    line,
That would be the signal to climb.

It's good to fly and be a kite;
Maybe some day I'll make a long
    flight.
The trouble begins when I'm caught
    in a storm:
If it's bad, I may come down torn.

I'm glad that I'm a free-flying kite —
The views that I see are a wondrous
    sight.
Some day when you see me pass by,
You'll wish that you were a kite in
    the sky.

      Scott Trevor, Age 12

Mice Are Pets?

Mice are small,
Mice are fat,
Mice make
    good pets for cats!

        Diana Taufer, Age 13

Mice

E-E-K!
Is
The noise
My mother
Makes when
She sees one!

      David Marsh, Age 13

Acknowledgments

Diligent effort has been made to trace the ownership of all copyrighted material and to obtain the necessary permissions to reprint these selections. If such acknowledgments have been inadvertently omitted, the compiler and publisher would appreciate receiving full information so that proper credit may be given in future editions.

Grateful acknowledgment is made to the following publishers, authors, and other copyright owners for permission to use the copyrighted selections in this book:

ABINGDON PRESS for "The Handiwork of God" and "Always Finish" by unknown authors on pages 136 and 145 of *Great Art and Children's Worship* by Jean L. Smith. Copyright 1948 by Stone and Pierce.

ASSOCIATION FOR CHILDHOOD EDUCATION INTERNATIONAL for "Fuzzy, Wuzzy, Creepy, Crawly" by Lillian Schulz Vanda from *Sung Under the Silver Umbrella*. Copyright 1935 by the Association for Childhood Education International.

ATHENEUM PUBLISHERS for "The Travelers" by Patricia Hubbell from *The Apple Vendor's Fair*. Copyright © 1963 by Patricia Hubbell.

MRS. PETRA CABOT for "The Little Man Who Wasn't There" by Hughes Mearns from *Creative Youth Anthology of Lincoln School Verse*.

CENTURY CO. for "The Little Elf" by John Kendrick Bangs from *St. Nicholas Book of Verse*. Copyright 1923 by The Century Company.

WILLIAM COLE for the poem beginning "It's such a shock, I almost screech" from *Rhyme Giggles*. Copyright © 1967 by William Cole.

GEORGE M. COHAN MUSIC PUBLISHING COMPANY for lyrics to "You're a Grand Old Flag" by George M. Cohan.

CONCORDIA PUBLISHING HOUSE for "Thank You, Jesus, for This Day," "My Savior, Hear My Prayer," and "Two Little Eyes" from *Little Children Sing to God!* Compiled and edited by A. H. Jahsmann and A. W. Gross and copyright © 1960 by Concordia Publishing House.

DODD MEAD & COMPANY for "The Owl and the Pussy-Cat," "They Went to Sea in a Sieve, They Did," "There Was an Old Man with a Beard," and "Twinkle, Twinkle, Little Bat," by Edward Lear from *The Complete Nonsense Book*.

DOUBLEDAY & COMPANY for "Circus Elephant" by Kathryn Worth Curry from *Poems for Josephine*. Copyright 1937 by Kathryn Worth Curry. For "Mice" by Rose Fyleman from *51 New Nursery Rhymes*. Copyright 1932 by Doubleday & Company. For "Only My Opinion" by Monica Shannon from *Goose Grass Rhymes*. Copyright 1930 by Doubleday & Company. For "Recessional" by Rudyard Kipling from *Favorites*. For "Fourth of July" by Rachel Field from *A Little Book of Days*. Copyright 1927 by Doubleday & Company. For "If" by Rudyard Kipling from *Rewards and Fairies*. Copyright 1910 by Rudyard Kipling.

E. P. DUTTON & COMPANY, INC. for "America the Beautiful" by Katharine Lee

189

WESTERN PUBLISHING COMPANY, INC. for "A Ballad of Johnny Appleseed" by Helmer O. Oleson from *Story Parade*. Copyright 1952 by Story Parade, Inc.

YALE UNIVERSITY PRESS for "Chanticleer" by John Farrer from *Songs for Parents*. Copyright 1921 by Yale University Press.

Grateful thanks is made to the following authors whose addresses, publishers, agents, and/or trustees I was unable to locate:

James Barton Adams for "The Cowboy's Life"; William Henry Davies for "Leisure"; F. E. Elwell for "Courtesy"; Edwina Fallis for "Wise Johnny"; Louis and Linka Friedman for "April Rain" ("The Rain Song" or "Song") by Robert Loveman; Esther Gillespie for "God Is Everywhere" and "Who Taught Them?" by unknown authors; Reginald Holmes for "Little Girl's Heart"; W. D. Howard for "Young Men!"; Ann Johnson for "Grandma"; Richard LeGallienne for "I Meant to Do My Work Today"; Mary Wright Saunders for "Remembering Day"; James Stephens for "The Wind"; Dorothy Brown Thompson for "Wish"; and Thomas H. B. Webb for "An Ancient Prayer."

Index of Titles and First Lines

*The first lines of Scripture are italicized

195

198

200

 Index of Authors and Sources

206